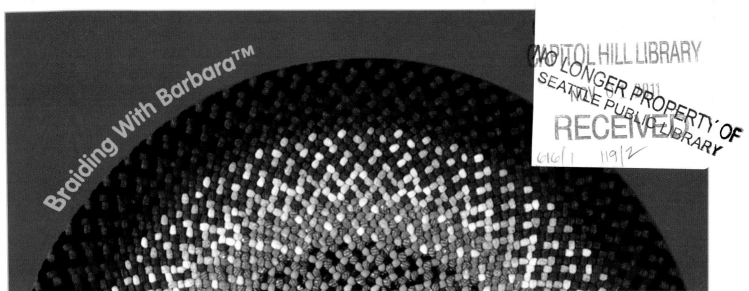

Braiding With Barbara™

Wool Rugs with a Contemporary Flair

Barbara A. Fisher & Janet A. Fitzgerald

Schiffer Publishing Ltd

4880 Lower Valley Road · Atglen, Pennsylvania 19310

D1571572

Schiffer Books are available at special discounts for bulk purchases for sales promotions or premiums. Special editions, including personalized covers, corporate imprints, and excerpts can be created in large quantities for special needs. For more information contact the publisher:

Published by Schiffer Publishing Ltd.
4880 Lower Valley Road
Atglen, PA 19310
Phone: (610) 593-1777; Fax: (610) 593-2002
E-mail: Info@schifferbooks.com

For the largest selection of fine reference books on this and related subjects, please visit our web site at **www.schifferbooks.com**
We are always looking for people to write books on new and related subjects. If you have an idea for a book please contact us at the above address.

This book may be purchased from the publisher.
Include $5.00 for shipping.
Please try your bookstore first.
You may write for a free catalog.

In Europe, Schiffer books are distributed by
Bushwood Books
6 Marksbury Ave.
Kew Gardens
Surrey TW9 4JF England
Phone: 44 (0) 20 8392 8585; Fax: 44 (0) 20 8392 9876
E-mail: info@bushwoodbooks.co.uk
Website: www.bushwoodbooks.co.uk

Dedication

I dedicate this book to my family.
They have always been so supportive through the past 50+ years of my rug braiding.

I also dedicate it to my hundreds of rug students who have given me so much joy watching them create their works of art.

Designed by RoS
Type set in VAG Rounded/Swiss 721 BT

ISBN: 978-0-7643-3458-0
Printed in China

Table of Contents

Introduction

Wool Rugs with a Contemporary Flair is a reference guide for both the beginner and advanced braider. This book explains the techniques for using the Counted Loop Method™ of braiding which was developed by Barbara Fisher and what you need to get started.

There are basically two methods to braiding rugs—spiral and butted. **Spiral rugs** are made of a single long braid that is wrapped around itself. **Butted rugs** are made of separate rings that are later laced together. You make these rings by braiding a straight braid then joining or butting the ends together to make a ring. Butting allows the braider more flexibility in applying designs for advanced geometric configuration, shapes, and custom color schemes. Spiral rugs are more restrictive when choosing color schemes and shapes. The greatest difference between these methods is that in the butting method you don't have to carry the rug with you when you are working on it, because each row is done separately, whereas the spiral rug is one long braid that is always attached to the rug.

You need to decide in the beginning which method you are going to use because the braiding is started slightly different for each method.

Happy Braiding!

Abbreviations Used in this Book

CLL	center line lacing
DEC	decrease
INC	increase
L	left
LAL	lace all loops
LBP	loops between each pin going down the curve
LME	loops between the pins in the exact middle ends
LP	loop
LS	light Solid
M	middle
MC	matching color
P	plaid
R	right
REV	reverse the open edges
SR	number of sets in a row

Chapter 1

Counted Loop Basics:
Tools, Planning, & Fabric Preparation

Tools & Supplies

Before beginning to braid, it is a good idea to have the following materials on hand:

- Notebook
- Sewing needles and thread
- Safety pins (11 small and 4 medium are needed for each butt)
  - ~50 Small (size 1)
  - ~25 Medium (size 2)
- Short common pins with large heads
- Sharp pointed scissors, 1 small and 1 large
- Needle-nose pliers
- Ruler & tape measure
- Spring-type clothespins
- Rubber bands, size 31
- White cardboard to use for tags
- 3" x 24" plain strip of white sheeting that can be written on
- Lacing needles – round and flat
- Lacing thread: #9 lockstitch that can be spliced
- Braiding clamp and/or stand
- Woolen fabric

The list of supplies above looks long at first glance, but you may already have many of these items in your home. The following pages contain a more detailed description of most of the items on the list.

I keep all my materials in a basket so they are readily at hand when I need them.

Notebook
It is always good to have a notebook handy. Writing things down is the best way of keeping track of special notes.

Safety Pins
Safety pins are used to mark the various steps when butting and are also used to attach tags identifying your rows. You will need two sizes, small and large.

Common Pins
Common pins are used to mark where "increases" and "decreases" are going to be made as the rows of braid are laced together. The pins should have large heads and short stems to make them easier to use.

Scissors
A small pair of scissors with sharp points are used to snip the wool when butting. A larger pair of scissors is useful for trimming and cutting the braids.

Needle-nose Pliers
Needle-nose pliers are used in butting and to pull loops back into place.

Ruler & Tape Measure
A small 6-inch ruler is handy for measuring the width of the strips. A tape measure is used to measure the width and length of the rug.

Spring-Type Clothespins
These clothespins are placed on the ends of the braid anytime you stop braiding to keep the braid from coming undone.

Rubber Bands (2-3 inches in length or size 31)
These are used to roll the wool strips. Rolling strips keeps them from tangling as they are braided. *See page 19.*

Heavy Paper for Tags
Old greeting cards, business cards, or index cards cut into 1-inch squares. These are used as tags to label your braids with row numbers, lacing instructions, and to mark the "wrong side" of the rug.

Strip of Cloth for Color-Scheme Plan
This can be a strip of white sheeting cut approximately 3" x 24" that can be written on.

Lacing Needle
The rounded tip of a straight, blunt-end darning needle, made of stainless steel and 2-3/4 inches long, enables you to lace your braided loops without catching the material. You also use this needle to splice pieces of the lacing thread together.

Curved Flat Needle
With this flat needle, it is easier to do your center line lacing without piercing the material.

Lacing Thread #9
This thread is especially good for lacing braided rugs. It has a tubular center that can be spliced, eliminating bulky knots. If you tie knots in your lacing thread, eventually the ends of the knot poke through the braid when you vacuum the rug. If you keep cutting off these ends, the knots will come untied and break open the rows of braid. By splicing the lacing thread together, all knots are eliminated and the rug is laced with one continuous thread.

This metal clamp attaches to the edge of the work table.

This type of clamp stands on the floor.

Braiding Clamp or Stand
A clamp or stand used to hold the end of your braid while you braid the strips of fabric. A braiding clamp is much easier to carry around, but you must have a table to which to clamp it. A braiding stand is helpful because you can carry it from room to room and use it without having to clamp it to a table. A new traveling metal stand tucks under your thigh allows you to sit anywhere and braid—even while a passenger in a car! All devices are meant only to hold your braid straight while braiding.

Woolen Fabric
The wool fabric is the most important ingredient of your rug. Because so much time and effort goes into making a rug, it should be made to last forever. Wool is the best material for rugs, but other types of fabric can be used—experiment and have fun with it!

Choosing Your Rug

As you plan your rug, it is a good idea to consider your level of braiding experience and skill. Of the two basic methods, butted and spiral, the spiral method is best suited for the beginning braider because it has one continuous braid rather than each row being a separate loop to be butted together. When the line of braid is finished, it is wrapped around itself in a spiral, leading away from the center.

While requiring more skill, butted construction has the advantage of convenience. A few rows can be worked on at a time before lacing. The rug can be left on a table in a work room and the braiding can be done anywhere—the kitchen, the living room, and even at a neighbor's house while enjoying good coffee and good company. When enough has been braided, it can be butted (joining the ends) and taken to the workroom, where it is laced on to the rug.

Similarly, ovals and circles are easier than squares, rectangles, hexagons, or other multi-sided rugs with turns. The best project for a beginner is either a small spiral oval mat with no color changes or a small all-butted oval mat.

A rug made of cotton strips with a flannel sheet filler.

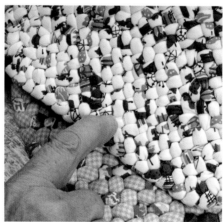

The blue and white rug is made of cotton without a flannel filler. You can see that it is less puffy.

This and the basket on page 46 used double knit polyester strips.

What Kind of Fabric?

Flannel weight fabric, preferably 100 percent wool and permanently mothproofed, is the very best kind to buy, but it is not always easy to find. This wool is easier to braid, makes a warmer rug, lasts longer than any other material, and makes a neater braid. A 100 percent wool rug stays much cleaner because the wool has lanolin in it. For instance, if you spill a cup of coffee on an all-wool rug, the coffee will roll off like water on a duck's back. However, on blends of wool and something else, spilled coffee will sink into the material and stain it before you can wipe it up.

Ready to braid wool can be purchased all stripped and rolled from the Braided Rug Shop. If you buy wool dressmaking fabric by the yard that feels stiff or wool that seems to have a loose weave, it may need to be washed before braiding.

When buying woolen scraps, be sure they are at least 85% wool, though 100% wool is the better choice. Scraps with the selvedge (finished) edges intact are best, because they provide you with a straight edge. Make sure the scraps are wide enough (1-3/4 to 2 inches) to allow for removal of the selvedge edge and a little shrinkage when washed.

Beautiful rugs have also been made from old clothing. Do not mix new wool with old wool in the same rug; the old wool will wear out before the new. If you are using old clothing, different colors and shades may be obtained from the same garment simply by dyeing the material.

If old clothing and material varies in thickness, cut the strips slightly wider when using thin material and narrower when using thick material. All woolen rugs can be either washed or dry cleaned.

Experimenting with other fabrics such as cotton, jersey, and double knits can lead to some interesting designs and textures. Be adventurous!

What Colors?

Colors say a great deal. They can be warm or cold, dangerous or dull, busy or quiet. Make the colors in your rug say what you want them to say. For example, for an autumn-colored rug, use three shades of green and three shades of brown, then add some excitement with gold, rust, and burnt orange.

For a blue rug you could use three shades of blue, three shades of gray, and then add a gold or terra-cotta for accent.

Most rugs are made from a mix of solid colors and patterned fabrics, such as plaids, tweeds, small checks, or herringbone. In this book, the term "plaid" refers to *any fabric that has a pattern that is not a solid color*. When planning a project, it is helpful to choose the plaid fabric first and then pick solid colors to match some of the colors in it.

Some hints:

• Checks, tweeds and herringbones are the best patterned fabrics to use when you start braiding rugs, because their patterns are small and even.

• Buy small plaids rather than large ones.

• Use neutral colors, like beige, gray, or brown, to tone down the brighter colors of your rug.

How Much Fabric?

It is important to know how much wool to buy at one time. If you are buying continually available yard goods, buy only what you need as you go along. For example, you could start with only 1/4 yard of each of your first three colors—a plaid, a dark solid, and a light solid. Remember, though, that the color shading varies somewhat between dye lots, and the next bolt the store brings in might be slightly different.

When buying scraps, purchase two or three pounds or several yards of each color at a time, especially when purchasing the plaids. Plaids are very hard to match if you should run out of them, so buy enough for the whole rug when you find a fabric you like. Unfortunately, the same fabric may never be available again.

After you have decided which size and shape your rug will be and plan the color scheme and any special color designs, the rug pattern will enable you to determine the amount of each color of wool to purchase.

Rug Size	Approx. Yardage
2' round	4
2' x 3'	6
3' x 5'	15
3' x 6'	18
4' x 6'	24
6' x 9'	54
5' x 11'	55
8' x 10'	80
9' x 12'	108

If you use 1-1/2" wide strips of wool, it takes approximately one yard of 54-inch wide wool fabric to make one square foot of rug. The following table shows the approximate number of yards of fabric needed to make various rug sizes:
Since there is a great deal of waste when using scraps, it takes approximately one pound of wool scraps for each square foot of rug. (1 lb = 1-1/2 yds of 54" wide flannel weight wool)

Matching Numbers & Sets:
Basic Units of Counted Loop Method™

A Braiding With Barbara™ rug pattern tells you how many rows of braiding are in the rug, how many "sets" are in each row, and how to lace the rows together. One "set" is 3 loops of braid so every third loop is the same color (see drawing). The patterns also explain how often to make turns in square, oval, heart, hexagon, octagon, and similar rugs.

The sets are counted using **Matching Color (MC) loops**. These get their name because they are used to align the rows of braids when the rug is laced up. Although any of the colors could be used as a matching color, the patterns in this book use the *dark solid loop* as the MC. As you lace the rows of braid together to assemble the rug, the MC loops in one row are aligned or "matched" with the MC loops in the next braided row.

To count the number of sets you need for a particular row, hold the braid with the right side facing up, as if you were braiding. In this position the 1st loop in the top right-hand position is a Matching Color (MC) loop, and the 4th loop down the right side is also an MC loop. When counting the sets, the top right-hand MC loop should be counted as zero. Since a set has three loops, one of each color, the next MC loop after MC#0 on the right edge makes one set, and every time an MC loop appears again on the right edge marks another set. Using this method of counting MC loops on the right hand edge of the braid, you can measure the number of sets called for by the pattern.

Note: In my patterns, the counting in the 1st row is measured by MCs rather than sets. For the center line, each "matching color" is counted, so the first matching color loop is "1" not "0."or "MCs."

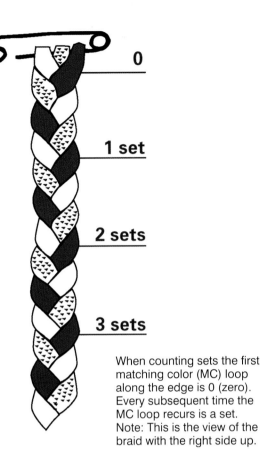

0

1 set

2 sets

3 sets

When counting sets the first matching color (MC) loop along the edge is 0 (zero). Every subsequent time the MC loop recurs is a set. Note: This is the view of the braid with the right side up.

Choosing the Pattern Size

Measure the area of the floor that you want the rug to cover when it is finished. The rug does not need to be an exact size. For example, a 2' X 3' oval rug will work nicely in a 2'3" X 3'5" space.

If the floor area is square then a round, square, hexagon or octagon pattern can be used. Some of these are quite advanced and, as a beginner, either an oval spiral with no color changes or an all butted oval should be the first project you consider.

With the basic measurement and a little mathematics, you can choose the right pattern size.

All the oval and rectangular patterns start with a certain number of sets in the center row. The length of this center row by subtracting the width from the total length. The 2' x 3' rug cited above, for example will have a center row of 1 foot.

To find how many sets are needed for the center row of the size rug you want, braid a strip 12" long and then count the number of matching color loops on the right-hand side of the braid, to determine the number of sets per foot. (Fig 1). Tightly braided, 1-1/2" wide strips of wool usually have 9 sets per 1 foot of braid. A 9' x 12' rug, then, would have a 3-foot center row (12' – 9'), and the center row would have 27 sets colors (3 x 9).

If a 2" wide strip is used, the braid will be larger and it may only take 7 sets to make one foot of braid.

Make your own 12" gauge of braid.

Common Rug Sizes

Here are some examples of very common rug sizes, with the number of rows in each one and the approximate yardage each takes:

Rug Size	Sq. ft.	Center row	Approx. yards	No. of rows
2' round	4	0	4	20
2' X 3'	6	9 sets	6	18
3' X 5'	15	18 sets	15	27
3' X 6'	18	27 sets	18	27
4' X 6'	24	18 sets	24	36
6' X 9'	54	27 sets	54	54
5' X 11'	55	54 sets	55	45
8' X 10'	80	18 sets	80	72
9' X 12'	108	27 sets	108	81

Special Cases

When measuring for a **chair pad**, subtract 1/2" from the overall measurement so that the chair pad will not come too close to the edge of the chair.

For **stair runners**, measure the width that the runner should be when it is finished. To get the length, measure one step and one riser then add these two together. Subtract 1/2" then multiply this number by the number of steps.

For example:

Step width	9"
Plus Step Riser	+7"
Sub Total	16"
Less	-0.5"
Total	**15.5"**
Total inches	15.5"
Times the number of stairs	x12
Finished length of runner	**186.0"**
Subtract the width of finished runner	-32"
Length of first row	**154.0"**

154.0" = 12' 10", the length of the center row

The length of the center row is used to determine the number of sets. If the gauge is 9 sets in one foot of braid, then the formula is 12 feet x 9 sets (108 sets) plus 10" more, which equals 118 sets for the center row of the stair runner

Planning the Color Pattern

It is a good idea to plan your color scheme before buying your wool. One handy tool is a color guide consisting of a long background strip of white sheeting on which you can write and fabric strips of the various colors you plan to use.

Cut several strips of each of the fabrics being used; make them about 1/2" long by 1-1/2" wide. The strip of white sheet should be about 3" wide and 24" or more in length, depending upon how large the rug pattern will be.

Decide what three-color combination will be used in the first row. Remember, two, or even all three colors, can be the same. At one end of the background strip, place the three fabric samples of the first color combination in an asterisk shape so they all show. While planning, use a common pin to secure the samples to the background.

Continue adding three-strip asterisks of until the color pattern is created. It is best to change just one color from color combination to the next, because it helps the colors to blend.

When you are satisfied with the color scheme, machine stitch all the asterisks to the background strip. Then refer to your pattern, decide the number of rows you want of each color combination, and write that information on the background strip beside the color asterisk.

Lay out the color scheme for the rug by applying pieces of the fabrics you intend to use on a strip of white sheeting. Starting at the top with the colors of the first row, make asterisks of the all the colors to be used in the rug. As you move from one asterisk to the next, change only one color, so the colors of the rug will blend. When you are satisfied with the color progression, stitch them in place and write the number of rows for each combination beside it on the sheet.

Estimate Yardage of Planned Colors

Once you have made up your color pattern and decided the size and shape of the rug you are going to make, you can figure out approximately how much of each color you have to buy for the whole rug.

Estimating yardage is easy to do with the Counted Loop Method™ but it does take some time.

If you use the normal 1-1/2" wide strips there is enough wool in 1/4 yard of 54" wide fabric to braid approximately 130 sets. You can easily tell how much wool to buy by counting the number of sets in each row of the pattern.

For example, let's say you need 1 strand of blue in each of the first four rows of the rug. The pattern calls for the following:

Row 1	42 sets
Row 2	44 sets
Row 3	46 sets
Row 4	50 sets

There are 23 color combinations for this rug, each represented by an asterisk.
The next job is to determine how many rows of each pattern will be used.

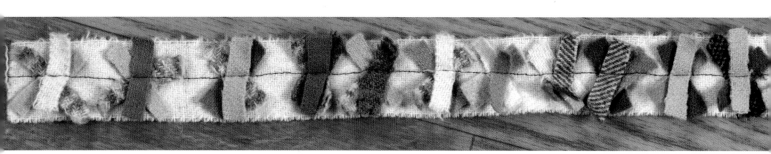

The color scheme for the rug in the photo.

That means you need 42+44+46+50=182 sets of the blue strand. To this **add 2 extra sets per row** (2 x 4=8) for butting:

$$182 + 8 = 190 \text{ sets.}$$

Divide this by 130 and the answer is 1 with a remainder of 60. You need 1/4 of a yard plus an additional amount to braid 60 more sets, which is a little less than 1/8 yard. This means you would be safe buying 1/4 yard + 1/8 yard (or 3/8 yard) of 54" wide blue wool.

Now let's say that in Row 4 you were going to use 2 strands of blue. So now the calculation would be 42+44+46+50+50=232, plus 10 (2 x 5) for the butting, making it a total of 242 sets.

Again you divide by 130. The result is nearly 2, so in order to make these 4 rows using 1 strand of blue in the first 3 rows and 2 strands of blue in the 4th row, you will need to buy 2/4 (1/2) yard of blue wool.

Note for Oval Rugs

On an oval rug pattern the 1st row just tells you how many MCs are in the center of the rug and not the final count of all the loops. **For calculating the wool needed in for row 1, use the same number of sets as in row 2.** For example, if the 1st row of an oval rug is 9MC and the 2nd row is 24 sets, then you need to use 24 sets for the both the 1st and 2nd row counts to calculate the wool needed. Also remember to add 2 extra sets to each row to do the butt.

Row 1, 9 MC: use 26 sets to calculate wool
Row 2, 24 sets: use 26 sets to calculate wool

Tricks & Tips for Estimating Fabric

Here are some other tricks and tips to help you plan how much wool you need. Remember that the exact gauge will depend on your own braiding style, how wide you cut the strips, and how loosely or tightly you braid.

• 10 rows of braid laced together will equal an approximately one-foot diameter round rug; 9 rows in an oval rug will produce a rug that is one foot across.

• A strip of 1-1/2" wide wool that is 1 yard long will make approximately 17 sets.

• 1/4 yard of wool will yield a strip of wool 9 yards long by 1-1/2" wide.

• If you have a roll of wool and you aren't quite sure it will be enough to go around the whole row when it is braided, unroll it and lay it around the rug. If it goes around 1-1/2 times unbraided, it will be long enough when it is braided to do the whole row.

• There are about 8 yards of braid, or approximately 200 sets, in 1 square foot of rug.

• 9 sets generally equal 1 foot of braid. This depends upon how you braid. After you develop consistency in the size of your braiding, measure one foot and count the sets.

Washing Wool Fabric

If you are going to wash or dye wool fabric do it before it is torn or cut. All wool scraps and any wool that has a sizing in it must be washed. Any wool that has been pressed flat should be washed to fluff it up. Loosely woven fabric should also be washed to strengthen it and pull the weave closer together. Most of the fabrics today do not require washing before using them.

While you should use very little soap when washing wool, adding 1 level teaspoon of soap to a washing machine full of water will reduce shrinkage. Put the wool in the washer and start it, but let it agitate for only about 3 minutes, just so that the soap has mixed through the wool to fluff it up. Turn the machine to rinse and let it rinse on the normal cycle. Dry the wool in the dryer or hang it up. It is perfectly fine to dry wool in the dryer. Heat is good because it fluffs up the fibers and makes plusher wool for braiding. Use a low heat setting and do not over dry.

Be careful not to shrink the wool too much by using too much soap. If it shrinks too much the wool becomes denser or thicker, so you need to cut the strips narrower than the regular strips to maintain the same braid size. With material that has been washed, it is a good idea to strip one piece and braid it to make sure of the size before you strip the whole piece of wool.

Dyeing Wool Fabric

Today, there are many methods for dyeing wool. This is a recipe that Barbara created early on, when good colors were not available. Today, with so many woolen mills closed, color choices are once again scarce. Consider dyeing wool as another task on your "Gee, I'd like to do that someday" list!

Dyeing

3 gallons water
1 tsp dry dye dissolved in 1 cup hot water
1/2 cup white distilled vinegar
1/2 level teaspoon powdered soap

Wash wool first using very little soap. Put it in the dye bath while wet, stir occasionally, and simmer for 20 minutes. Dye only 1 pound of wool at a time.

Removing Color

1 lb Wool
3 gals of water
1/2 level tsp soap powder

Simmer 20 minutes. You can use this water to tint a plaid by adding 1/2 cup of white vinegar.

To Tint Wool or Dull It

3 gals of water
1/2 level tsp soap powder

There are two methods for a darker tint or dulling of wool. One involves simmering a strip of black wool in 3 gallons of water for 10 minutes before removing the wool. The other use 1/8 teaspoon of brown dye instead. If you want a lighter shade, you can add a very small amount of color by wetting a toothpick, dipping it in dry dye, simmering it in the water as above, and remove. The soap is very important to insure even dyeing.

Add 1/2 cup white vinegar to water then 1-pound of the wool to be tinted. Be sure to wash the wool first.

Stripping Wool Fabric

Decide on the size of braid to want to use. To make a fine braid, cut the strips 1-1/2" wide. This is the most popular width and the easiest to braid. For thicker braids, strips can also be cut or torn to 1-3/4" wide or 2" wide, but strips that are wider than 2" will not work well.

All the patterns and rug sizes used with the *Braiding With Barbara*™ *Counted-loop Method*™ are based on the strips that are 1-1/2" wide. If you wish, patterns and rug sizes can also be used with wider width strips by converting the number of sets per foot. Instead of 9 sets per foot that the 1-1/2" strips produce, 2" strips produce approximately 7 sets per foot, and 1-3/4" strips produce about 8 sets per foot.

Some materials may be torn into strips and some must be cut. Test a piece to see if it tears smoothly and easily on either the crosswise or lengthwise grain. If it is loosely woven (as many plaids and tweeds are), or if it ravels easily when you tear it, you will need to cut it hand cut.

When cutting the strips, be sure to measure and cut the strips evenly; if you do not, the size of the braid will vary. When material can be torn, measure 1-1/2" from the even edge, snip it with scissors, then tear the strips. Measuring from the fuzzy edge will change the size of the strip.

 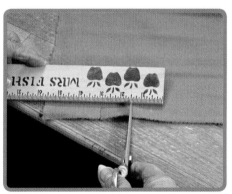 

To make fabric strips, measure from the selvedge edge, which will give you the straightest tear. The first strip includes the selvedge and will be 2-1/2" wide. Measure and make a snip.

The other strips will be 1-1/2" wide. Measure from the previous snip and make another snip.

Continue across the fabric.

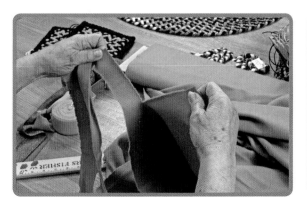 

From there it is just a matter of tearing the strips, starting at the snip.

Working with a friend will make short work of it.

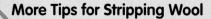

More Tips for Stripping Wool

• When one piece of material seems to be a little thicker, cut the strips a little narrower than the others.

• If a piece of wool seems to be a little thinner, cut it a little wider than normal. This will even out the bulk or thickness of the braids.

• Selvedge edges may be used if they are the same color and are not any thicker than the rest of the fabric.

• Rugs made with heavy wool coating fabric need to be stripped at least 1-3/4" to 2" wide; otherwise it will be to hard to fold in the edges

The thicker strip on the left has been cut a little bit narrower than the thinner strip on the right.

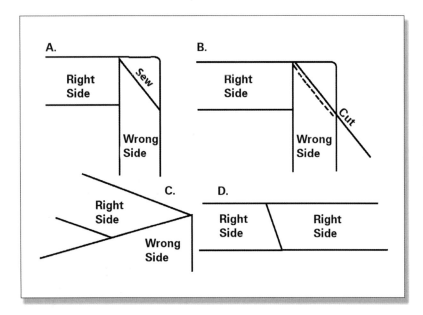

A. Lay one strip on the table with the right side facing up. Place the second strip on top with the right side down, forming an L. Sew the pieces together across the corner.
B. Cut off the corner.
C. Open the strip.
D. The result

Joining the Strips Together to Make a Roll

When the strips have been cut, you need to join the strips together end to end to create a long strip for braiding. To make the joint place the first strip down on the table with the right side of the material facing up. Place a new strip on top, with the right side facing down, forming an upside-down L with the right sides face each other (Fig 3-A). Sew the strips together on the bias across the corner, then trim off the corners (Fig 3-B). Unfold the strip (Fig 3-C) and you will have the two strips joined together with the right side facing up (Fig 3-D).

When working with plaids that have an obvious design (Fig 4), keep the different parts of the plaid on separate rolls.

In this example:

• The 1st and 6th strip are the same so they can be sewed on the same roll.

• The 2nd and 5th strips match each other and can be sewn on the same roll.

• Strips 3 & 4 can be joined as shown.

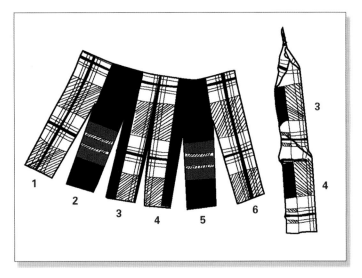

When making strips from plaid fabrics, try to match the pattern in the strip. Here 1 & 6 go together, as do 2 & 5 and 3 & 4.

Rolling the Strips on Rubber Bands

Once you have joined several strips, roll the wool on rubber bands so that it can be unrolled as it is braided. Open up the rubber band and start winding one end of the wool strip on to one side of the rubber band. Make sure that the right side of the wool is facing out and that the seams are facing the inside of the roll.

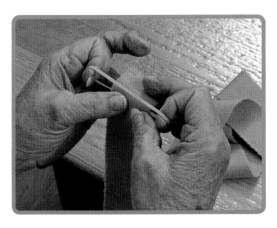

Use your thumb and middle finger to roll the strip around one side of the rubber band.

Rolling the strip on the rubber band begins by stretching the rubber band between your two forefingers, and running the end of the strip of fabric through the middle.

When you have a good amount, switch hand positions so the rubber band is stretched between the thumb and forefinger of one hand, and continue rolling the fabric using the other hand.

The result is a tightly held roll of fabric that easily unwinds as you need it.

Do the same for all the fabrics in your braid.

Chapter 2

How to Braid

Folding

The strips must be folded before they are braided

1. With the wrong side of the fabric up, fold the left side of the wool 3/4 of the way over to the right side.

2. Fold the right side back to the center.

3. Fold the whole braid in half.

This creates 5 layers of wool and keeps the braid round. Keep the open edges to the left side except when making the reverse braid on the last row.

When braiding, keep one of the rolls short and the others long. This will help keep them from tangling.

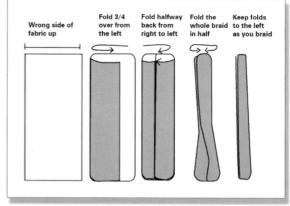

This diagram shows the basic folding technique.

With the wrong side of the fabric facing up, fold the left edge 3/4 of the way over.

Fold the right edge back over the left. It will go halfway across the strip.

Fold strip in half, so the open edge is on the left.

Placing Colors on a Safety Pin to Begin Each Row

When beginning to braid it is imperative to match the colors. As you are learning to braid, it is best to use 3 different colors: a light solid, a plaid, and a dark MC.

Referring to the color pattern strip for your rug design, you can place the folded fabric on a different safety pin for the start of each braid.

The normal rule of thumb for the first row is:

• the dark solid (MC) strip goes on the pin first, so it will be on the right

• the plaid (P) or tweed strip is second (middle)

• the light solid strip (LS) goes on the pin last (left).

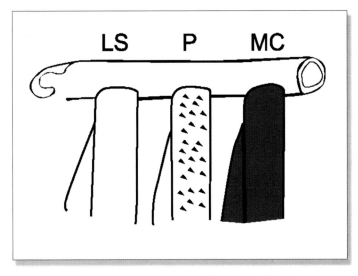

The order of colors on the pin. The matching color goes on first, followed by the plaid and the light solid.

The matching color, usually the dark solid, goes on the safety pin first. When it is folded, place it on the pin and slide it to the right.

Fold the dark solid color strip as described earlier. With the head of the safety pin to the left, place the dark solid strip on the pin so the seam is on the left, then slide it to the right.

Fold the plaid color or second strand the same way, and place it on the pin.

Finally, fold the light solid color or third strand the same way, place it on the pin, and snap the pin shut.

Make sure the open seams are all on the left side of the strand. Also make sure the colors are on the pin in the right order – MC on the right side, P in the middle, and LS on the left side as shown (Fig. 6).

The plaid strip is next. Fold as before, 3/4 of the way over from the left...

...back from the right...

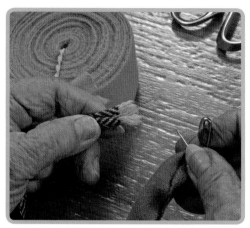
...and fold it in half.

Place it on the pin and slide it to the right.

The light solid is last. Fold it as before, 3/4 of the way form the left...

...back from the right...

...and fold it in half.

Place the light solid on the pin.

With the three strips on the pin, you are ready to braid.

When the pattern is set on the pin, write the combination on a piece of paper. For example:

Row 1: White–Plaid–Blue

Now you can follow the color pattern and create a safety pin for each row. If the next row in your color pattern uses some of the same colors as this row, write those colors directly underneath their matching color.

For example, if the color combination in Row 1 is white, plaid, and blue, as above, and your second color combination uses plaid, blue, and red, in Row 2 write blue on the right under blue, and the plaid in the center under the plaid. The new color, in this case red, will go on the left side, as shown below. As mentioned before, it is best to change just one color from one row to the next to help the colors blend.

This form has been designed to keep track of the order of colors, row by row. It has columns for Row #, Light Solid, Plaid, Dark Soild, and # of sets.

Row 1:	White	Plaid	Blue
Row 2:	Red	Plaid	Blue
Row 3:	Red	Plaid	Brown
Row 4:	Red	White	Brown
Row 5:	Yellow	White	Brown
Row 6:	Yellow	Plaid	Brown
Row 7:	Yellow	Plaid	New Color

The purpose of this placement pattern is to have the colors that are the same from row to row touch each other and create a pattern.

Each row will have its own safety pin and the color on the right goes on the safety pin first, followed by the other two in order.

If two strips in your color combination are to be the same, the odd color is the matching color (MC) and should be put on the pin as shown.

Placing Designs in a Braided Rug

Geometric designs can be created by repeating colors from row to row and by placing the strips on the safety pin in a certain order so that the repeated colors match up from one row to the next when the rows are laced together.

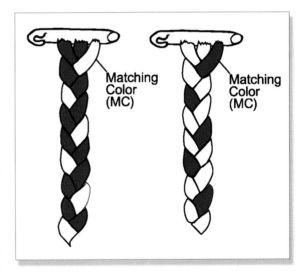

In these two braid examples, two colors are the same and the odd color is used as the matching color.

Examples of the types of geometric designs that can be made.

Braiding is the same for a spiral or butted rug, except that you start the braid differently.

Right Side of Braid

The ends of the strands for a butted rug are raw.

Right Side of Braid -Spiral

For a spiral rug the ends should be enclosed.

For a butted rug, you start braiding with the raw ends of the fabric on a safety pin because you will butt the ends together later.

For a spiral rug, you need to enclose the ends of the three strands before you start to braid so that you won't have any frayed ends showing in the center of your rug (Fig. 10).

For now, let's learn to braid by starting as if you were making an all-butted rug, using three pieces of fabric all of different colors (Fig. 9): a dark solid (your matching color or MC), a plaid (P), and a light solid color (LS). The side of the braid that is facing you is the right side of the rug.

As you braid, it is important to make sure the fold in the strip of fabric is maintained. I call that "fixing" the strand.

First, fix the fold on the right MC strand and secure it with your fingers. Next fix the fold on the left (LS) strand, and braid it over the middle (Fig 9 & Fig 10). The hand motion is important for keeping the fold in place: fix the fold, pick the strand up, and lift it over the middle strand, keeping your thumbs on top. This hand motion will keep your open seams to the left and keep the braid from twisting. **Do not pull tightly.**

Next, braid the right hand strand (the matching color, usually the dark solid) over the light solid which is now in the middle. Then the plaid, which is on the left, is carried over the master color, now in the middle.

As I am braiding, I say to myself: *Fix the right and hold; fix the left and braid, braid.*

The pattern continues left over middle, right over middle, left over middle, etc. etc., until the braid is completed.

Again, DO NOT PULL TIGHTLY. Braid closely together, but not tightly. Your braid is like an elastic band. If you pull it tightly and then braid, it is going to snap and break much sooner than if you just leave it relaxed while braiding. By pulling your braid tight, you are making your rug wear out even before it is on the floor.

In the beginning, braid slowly; speed will come with practice. Keep checking to see that the open seams are on the left edge of braid. By keeping them all to one side, you will be able to hide the open seams when you lace the rug together, making the rug reversible. Quality is more important than quantity and it is much better to do a little right than a lot wrong.

Also check for little folds in the fabric in your braid. These will appear if you aren't keeping that left side of the strip 3/4 of the way over to the right. This means you are not rolling the braid round enough, because you are flattening it out too much or are using material that is too thin.

The key to successful braiding is uniformity.

At the end of each braid, use your thumb hold it together while you are fixing the next braid. When you have braided two or three inches of braid, then move the last finished braid up to the braiding clamp or stand.

When you want to stop, place a clothespin over the last braid to hold it in place until you are ready to start again.

Fix the fold on the right matching color, so the opening is facing left.

Hold it securely.

Fix the fold on the plaid strand...

... and hold it securely.

Fix the fold of the left, light solid strand.

To braid, lift the strand straight up and bring it over and on top of the middle strand, keeping your thumb on top. This will keep the opening on the left and make an even braid.

Braid the left, light solid, strand over the middle, plaid, strand...

...then braid the right, dark solid, strand over the light solid.

Continue the braid, fixing the right folds, fixing the left folds, the braiding left over middle...

...and right over middle.

After you get the braid started a clamp or stand will make the work much easier. Remember to lift the strands straight up, thumbs on top...

... and lay them down so the opening stays on the left. The braids should be close, but not tight. Braiding too tightly will stretch the fabric and put stress on the braid, ultimately leading to a shorter life.

Note: A braiding stand or clamp will hold your braid in a straight line and make it much easier for you to manage your three strands without trying to keep the finished braid out of your way at the same time. Take the braid out of the clamp when you are making a turn.

Last Row-Reverse Braiding

On the last row of your rug, place the strands on the pin according to the color order from your planning sheet. Braid left over the middle to start but keep your open folds to the right and not to the left as when you normally braid. This is called reverse braiding.

For the last row, the opening of the strands on the needle is on the right. This is called reverse braiding.

Braiding Tips to Remember

If this is your first time using the Counted Loop Method™ of rug braiding, here are a few important do's and don'ts.

• Unless told otherwise, always start your colors as in the drawing on page 24, Light solid (LS)—Plaid (P)—Dark Solid (MC)

• Always keep one roll or strand shorter than the other two so that your wool rolls or strips will not get tangled.

• Always start your braid putting the left light solid (LS) over the middle plaid (P) first. If you don't, confusion may follow. For example, when the directions say to start your turn with the MC, your color will not match if you have not started your rug correctly.

• The reason for going by colors is to help you follow the pattern. If the pattern says the next loop should be the plaid and it isn't, that means you have made a mistake. Always check the last thing you did before going on.

• Braid with the open edges to the left. Only the last row is braided with the open edges to the right (usually called the reverse braid).

• While you are braiding, keep in mind that you are rolling your strands round instead of folding them flat. Roll them round like a pencil before you cross them over.

• Once you have started, never change the size of your braid. This causes bumps and ruffles. Set your gauge and stick to it.

• Braid the strips close together, but do not braid tightly or pull the braid towards you. Try to think of it as placing the strips side to side. Pulling the braid toward you makes a long, narrow braid, while you want a short, fat braid. DON'T BRAID TIGHTLY—give your rug a chance to breathe.

• Never iron out a bump. They can easily be fixed by lacing.

Do not get discouraged or impatient. You are teaching your hands to do something they have never done before, so give them a chance to practice. Like playing the piano, you have to practice before you can play well.

Chapter 3

The Perfect Butt™

Butting means joining the two ends of a single braid to complete a ring or square. The most important part of butting is having the right size safety pins and placing them in the correct spots and in the correct way.

For each butt you will need:

- 11 small pins
- 4 large pins

Organize the pins before starting:

- 1 small pin: the *pin end* pin, used to start the braid
- 1 small pin: *wrong side* pin
- 6 small pins: *snipping* pins
- 1 small pin with 1 small pin attached: *small stopper* pin
- 1 large pin with 1 small pin attached: *big stopper pin*
- 1 large pin: *matching color* pin
- 1 large pin: *one-more-time* pin
- 1 large pin: *holding* pin

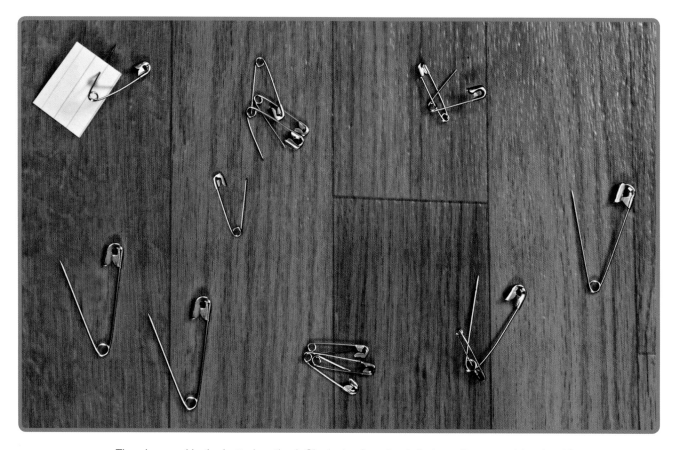

The pins used in the butted method. Clockwise from top left: 1 small **wrong side pin** with tag; 1 small **end pin**; 3 **snipping pins**; 1 **small stopper pin** (small pin with a small pin attached); 1 large **matching color pin**; 1 **big stopper pin** (large pin with small pin attached); 3 **snipping pins**; 1 large **one-more-time pin**; 1 **holding pin**

It is very helpful to make a small sample showing the placement of pins that you can keep as a model. To do this, make a braid that is 11 sets long, using a dark solid, a plaid, and a light solid, then follow steps 1-5 below. Stop after step five, leave the pins in the braid, and set aside. Keep this sample in your braiding basket to copy each time you butt. Referring to this sample every time you butt will save you from trying to remember all the pins.

A braid has two ends, a beginning end with a safety pin in it (the *pin end*), and an end held together with a clothespin (the *clothespin end*).

Note: Do not enclose the ends of the strands. Butted braids require open ends for joining; enclosed ends are only done when making spiral rugs. Just place your three strips on a *pin end* safety pin in the right order, leaving the ends of your wool open.

Make the braid in the way described earlier. With the right side facing up, begin by braiding the left light solid over the middle plaid, and continue to the desired length.

STEP 1: Butting is done on the wrong side of the braid. This is the underneath side that you cannot see when you are braiding.

Mark the wrong side of your braid by placing a small *wrong side* pin. The *wrong side* pin should have a tag that has the row number, the number of sets in the row, and the lacing instructions, as specified in the pattern. Keep this pin away from the area where you will be butting so you will not confuse it with your butting pins.

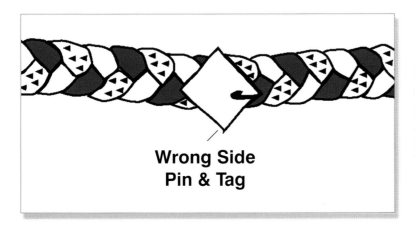

**Wrong Side
Pin & Tag**

Place a wrong side pin on the back of the braid. This should have the row number, the lacing instructions, and the number of sets in the row, as specified by the pattern.

Note: Remember, if this is the last row of your rug, braid with the open edges to the right instead of to the left. This is called reverse braiding.

Pin End

0
1
2
3
4
5
6
7
8
9

Clothespin End

STEP 2: With the pin end in your left hand and the right side of the braid facing up, count the number of sets you need for a particular row on the right-hand edge of the braid, as described earlier. Remember to add 2 extra sets to the count for the butt end. So if the pattern calls for 9 sets, braid 11.

Hold the pin end with your left hand and the hold the counted (from the pattern) MC loop (matching color loop) in your right. The 2 added sets will be beyond this counted loop.

Working on a table top, turn the left hand end upside down on the table in front of the braid..

Put your counted MC loop over and on top of zero loop at the beginning of the braid and pin the two loops together using the large *matching color* **pin**. You now have a ring of braid joined together through one MC loop from the *pin end* and one MC loop from the *clothespin end*. And we are now working from the wrong side of the rug (Fig. 15x)

The two ends of the braid are referred to as the *pin end* (shown here)...

...and the *clothespin end,* seen here under my right hand. Lay the braid on the table so the pin end is in you left hand, and the right side is up. Count the number of sets the pattern specifies for the row, along the edge, using matching colors and hold the braid there. Remember the first matching color (the one that is pinned) is zero. For this row the pattern calls for 9 sets, so I count 9 MCs from the pin end. (Remember the row needs 2 additions sets for the butt.)

Lift the pin end off the table...

...and fold it over so it is upside down and the right side is against the table.

Place the counted MC loop in your right hand, over the "zero" loop on the pin end.

Pin the loops together using the large **matching color pin**.

STEP 3: Next, add the big stopper pin. At the clothespin end, count over one MC loop to the right from the *matching color* pin and place the **big stopper *p*in** (a large safety pin with a small pin attached) through the whole braid, If you aim the pin up and to the right you catch loops of all three strands starting in the plaid, going through the light solid, and ending up in the matching color. If you aim it to the left, you will pick up the wrong loops. When you close this pin make sure it has come out through the MC loop. This is the *big stopper **p**in*.

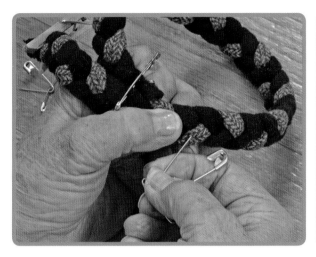 

Count over 1 MC loop to the right and insert a **big stopper pin** (a big safety pin with a small pin attached.) The pin should go through the whole braid, so it will hold it together when you open up the end. If you start in the plaid and aim up and to the right...

...you will go through the light solid and the dark solid (MC) loops.

STEP 4: On the pin end, at the beginning of the braid, count two MC loops to the left of the *matching color* pin put a **small stopper pin** (a small safety pin with another small pin attached) through just two loops, the plaid and the matching color. Again aim your pin up and to the right, and make it come out through the matching color. I have named these two pins "stopper pins" because they will stop you at the right place when you open your braid to finish your butt. Never remove the stopper pins until the butt is finished and you have recounted your loops to be sure you have right number.

To the left of the **matching color pin** (toward the pin end), count 2 MC loops place a **small stopper pin.** Again, aim up and to the right picking up all three strands and coming out through the MC loop.

The MC pin, big stopper pin, and small stopper pin in place.

STEP 5: Again, start from the *matching color* pin on the clothespin end and follow the MC strand under the light solid loop toward the clothespin. It will go under the light solid and come up again on the outer edge of the ring. Just where the MC strand starts to show, place a small safety pin, aiming it to the left. This is the first **snipping pin**. In the same way, place another small safety pin in each of the next two loops on the outer edge of the ring, moving toward the clothespin. You now have a small safety pin in each of the three colors on the outer edge of the braid. These pins mark the spots where you later will snip a hole in the wool. They are called **snipping** pins.

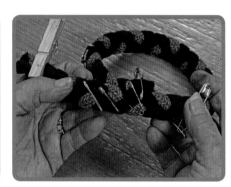

Next we add **snipping pins**. Starting at the MC pin, follow the MC strand toward the clothespin. It will go under the light solid loop and come out again on the outer edge of the ring. Just where it emerges from the light solid loop, place a small snipping pin in it aiming up and to the left.

Now place a **snipping pin** in each of the next two loops, moving along the outer edge toward the clothespin. Follow the same angle.

When you are done you will have a **snipping pin** in each color loop.

Three more small *snipping* pins are placed on the pin end of the braid. The first is on the edge of the MC loop (the same loop that your *MC pin* is in) just before it goes underneath the next loop to the left, away from the *matching color* pin. Make sure this is in the matching color loop with the matching color pin. Go straight back with the pin, then place two more pins in the next two loops in the same way. Like the other snipping pins, each will be in one of the three colors They are on the top or inner edge of the braid and mark the place where the wool will be snipped.

Three snipping pins are place on the pin end of the braid. The first is on the edge of the MC loop, just before it goes under the next loop. Go straight back with the pin.

Place a second snipping pin on the edge of the next loop...

...and a third on the edge of the next. There should now be a snipping pin in a loop of each color at the pin end.

Now is a good time to check the locations of your *wrong side* pin with the tag. This wrong side pin can be anywhere between the *small stopper* pin and the *big stopper pin*. Keep it far enough away from each, so as not to confuse it with your stopper pins.

Move the wrong side pin so it is away from both ends and out of the way.

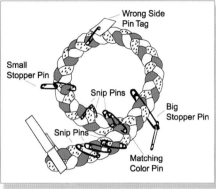

This drawing shows the location of the pins as we get ready to butt.

[**Note:** If you are making this braid for a sample, stop here and put it aside for reference.]

STEP 6: To continue the butting, make six snips in the braid where you have placed the six small snipping pins. On the pin end, snip against the snipping pin but just to the right. Always start with the matching color loops, followed by the two loops to the left. On the clothespin end, snip against the pin and just to the left.

As there name implies, each snipping pin marks a spot where a snip will be made. The snip then will mark where the strand will be cut in preparation for butting. At the pin end, snip against the pin and just to the right. Snip at each pin.

On the clothespin end snip against the pin and just to the left.

35

STEP 7: Remove the six *snipping* pins, the *MC pin*, the *pin-end* pin, and the clothespin. DO NOT REMOVE THE LARGE & SMALL STOPPER PINS. Undo the braid from both ends back to the *stopper pins*. If you have undone the braid enough and placed the *stopper pins* correctly, the colors will be opposite each other. The MCs will both be at the top of the braid and the plaid color will be at the bottom, and the light solid will be in the middle

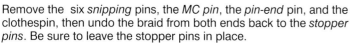

Remove the six *snipping* pins, the *MC pin*, the *pin-end* pin, and the clothespin, then undo the braid from both ends back to the *stopper pins*. Be sure to leave the stopper pins in place.

If you have undone the braid enough and placed the *stopper pins* correctly, the colors will be opposite each other. The MCs will both be at the top of the braid and the plaid color will be at the bottom, and the light solid will be in the middle

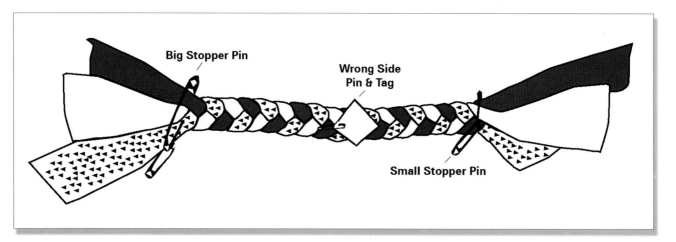

In this diagram you can clearly see that the strands match up. Notice that on the top and bottom strands one side has a short tail and the other long, and that on the middle strand the tails are equal. This helps keep things straight when you are using two strands of the same color.

STEP 8: Start at the *big stopper pin* end of the braid, turning the braid so the end is facing you. Open up one of the three strands of wool, keeping the right side of the fabric facing up. Holding the wool directly in front of you, find the snip. Align the scissors straight across the snip, then pivot them counterclockwise 1/2" and cut, as shown. Do the same on the other two strands at the *big stopper pin* end.

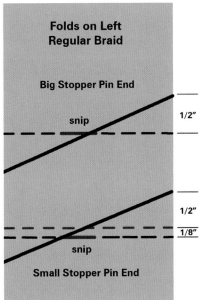

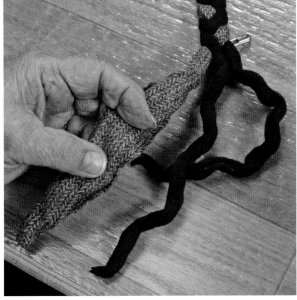

Next we are going to open the ends of the strands and cut across them at an angle through the snips we made. The too ends are treated slightly differently, as shown in this drawing.

At the *big stopper pin* end of the braid, turning the braid so the end is facing you. Open up one of the three strands of wool, keeping the right side of the fabric facing up. Holding the wool directly in front of you, find the snip.

Align the scissors straight across the snip...

...then pivot them counterclockwise 1/2" and cut.

Do the same on the other two strands at the *big stopper pin* end.

Turn the braid so the *small stopper pin* end is facing you. Open a strand, keeping the right side of the fabric facing up. Align the scissors and pivot just as you did on the previous cut, but move the scissors 1/8" above the snip before cutting. Do the same with the other two strands on the *small stopper pin* end. Check the angle.

Turn the braid so the *small stopper pin* end is facing you.

Open a strand, keeping the right side of the fabric facing up. Align the scissors...

...and pivot just as you did on the previous cut, but move the scissors 1/8" above the snip before cutting.

Do the same with the other two strands on the *small stopper pin* end. Go straight across the snip...

...pivot the scissors 1/2" counter-clockwise...

...shift the scissors 1/8" inch toward the braid and cut.

When you lay the braid on the table with the wrong side up, you will notice that the MCs are still at the top, and the one on the right has a long tail and the one on the left has a short tail. The plaid strands are at the bottom, with the left one having a long tail and the right a short tail. The two middle strands are both medium lengths. If you were butting braids with three strands of the same color, this pattern of varying lengths would make it easier to match up the different strands for the next step.

STEP 9: As shown in the drawing, the matching colors at each end will be sewn together. Being careful not to twist the wool, first put the ends of the MC strands together so the right sides are face to face and the ends aligned. Make a 1/4 inch seam, no more–no less, because this allowance was made when the wool was cut. Trim to 1/8". Next sew the other outside strands together the same way. DO NOT SEW the middle strands yet.

Note: If you are butting with three strands of the same color wool and do not have colors to use for matching, then you go by the long and short ends as described above. Sew the short tail of one end to the long tail of the other, and the long tail one end to the short tail of the other. Do not sew your middle tails together yet.

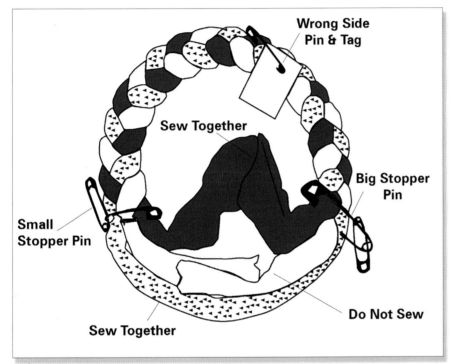

A drawing showing how the strands are joined together in a butt. Note that the middle strands are not joined until after the braiding is complete.

Being careful not to twist the wool, first put the ends of the MC strands together so the right sides are face to face and the ends aligned.

Make a 1/4 inch seam, no more–no less, because this allowance was made when the wool was cut.

Trim to 1/8".

The outside strands are matched and sewn in the same way.

Trim in the same way. DO NOT SEW the middle strands yet.

STEP 9a: Re-fold the strand at the joining seam and blind stitch by hand the folded edge about 1/2 to each side of the seam to hold it together.

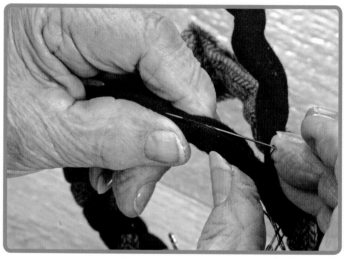

Re-fold the MC strand at the joining seam...

...and blind stitch by hand the folded edge about 1/2 to each side of the seam to hold it together.

Refold and blind stitch the plaid strand in the same way.

Refolded and ready for rebraiding.

STEP 10: Re-braiding starts from the *big stopper pin* end. Hold the braid so the right side is facing up and the *big stopper pin* is on the wrong side of the braid. Braid until the unsewn tail ends up on the right hand edge of the braid. When it does, make one more braid from the left over the middle (a plaid color) and pin it in that position. This pin is called the **one-more-time** pin (see the drawing) which holds the plaid in the middle so it doesn't move when making the butt. When someone says their butt doesn't work, it's usually because they forgot the "one more time pin."

When placing the one more time pin from right to left, take a bite from the light solid, press down on the plaid loop before going through it, then grab a bite of the matching color loop.

Hold the braid so the right side is facing up and the *big stopper pin* is on the wrong side of the braid.

Braid as usual...

...until the unsewn tail ends up on the right hand edge of the braid.

When it does, make one more braid from the left over the middle (a plaid color) and pin it in that position. This pin is called the **one-more-time** pin (see the drawing), which holds the plaid in the middle so it doesn't move when making the butt. When someone says their butt doesn't work, it's usually because they forgot the "one more time pin."

When placing the one more time pin from right to left, take a bite from the light solid, press down on the plaid loop before going through it, then grab a bite of the matching color loop.

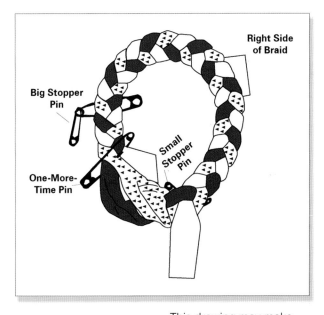

This drawing may make these steps a bit clearer.

STEP 11 : Flip the braid so the wrong side is up. The *small stopper pin* will be on top. Braid from the *small stopper pin* end (see the drawing). You will then notice the middle strand is not caught in the pin, so give it an extra pull before you start to re-braid it. Braid until the two unsewn tails meet. Remove the *one-more-time pin*. Make sure the two open edges are facing you, then place the two unsewn tails face to face. Sew a 1/4" seam, then trim to 1/8".

Pull all your loops back into shape and check to see if there are ten loops between the *stopper pins* including stopper pin loops.

Before removing the stopper pins, make sure you have a tag on the wrong side (the same side we just did the butting on) telling you which row it is and the number of sets it has in the row and the lacing instructions from the pattern.

Flip the braid so the wrong side is up. The *small stopper pin* will be on top. Braid from the *small stopper pin* end. (Figure 41) You will then notice the middle strand is not caught in the pin, so give it an extra pull before you start to re-braid it.

Braid until the two unsewn tails meet.

Remove the *one-more-time pin*.

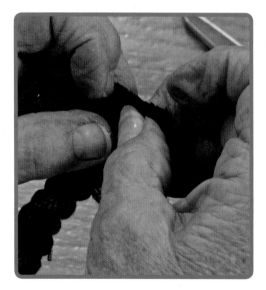

Make sure the two open edges are facing you, then place the two unsewn tails face to face.

Sew a 1/4" seam...

...then trim to 1/8".

Pull all your loops back into shape and check to see if there are ten loops between the *stopper pins* including stopper pin loops. (see drawing)

Needle nose pliers are helpful when reshaping the braid.

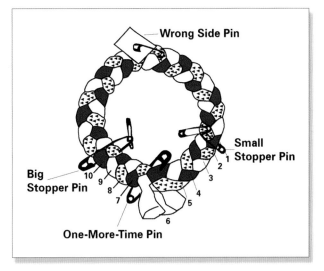

Drawing showing the butt just before the last strand is sewn. Each loop is counted, including those with the stopper pins. Before removing the stopper pins, make sure you have a tag on the wrong side (the same side we just did the butting on) telling you which row it is and the number of sets it has in the row and the lacing instructions from the pattern.

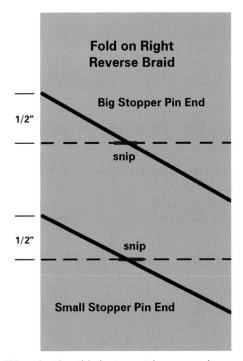

When butting this last row, trim your snips at the opposite angle, turning your scissors clockwise. Do not go up 1/8" on the small stopper pin end on the reverse braid.

Butting the Last Row

The last row of the rug was reverse braided, using the same steps as usual, but with the open edges to the right instead of to the left.

When butting this last row, trim your snips at the opposite angle, turning your scissors clockwise. Do not go up 1/8" on the small stopper pin end on the reverse braid.

Congratulations, you have finished "The Perfect Butt"™. Remember that old saying, "practice makes perfect"!

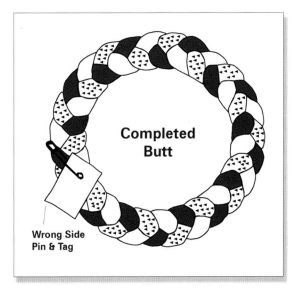

The completed butt

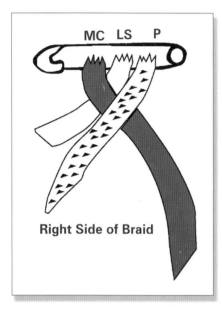

MC   LS   P

Right Side of Braid

Strand order for a 2-MC
oval center

Occasionally you need to modify the regular method of butting to accommodate special situations such as when the butt requires a small number of MCs (matching colors), less fabric, or all the same color. In this section you will learn how to butt a 2 MC center row for an oval shape and how to use it to make a basket, a special way to make the center for a square shape using the same color wool, and a 9 loop center for making a round or hexagon center.

Butting a 2-MC Oval Center, Row 1

• Place 24" long strips on the pin starting with the plaid, then the light solid, and the dark solid (MC). Braid left over the middle first.

• Braid until you have a count of 6 loops on the left edge.
• Braid the first turn
  – Start with the MC on the left in your left hand
  – Braid left over the middle with the MC
  – Braid left over the middle again with the light solid
  – Braid right over the middle with the plaid
  – Braid left over the middle with the MC
  – Braid left over the middle with the plaid
  – Braid right over the middle with the light solid.

• Braid 6 more loops counting them on the left edge.

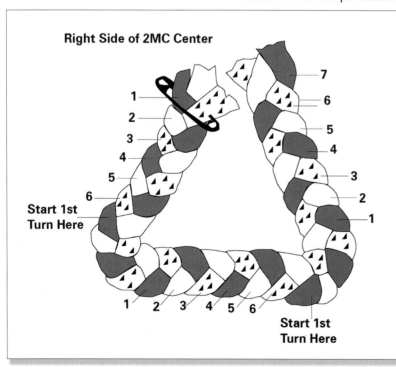

Right Side of 2MC Center

1 2 3 4 5 6 7

Start 1st Turn Here

1 2 3 4 5 6

Start 1st Turn Here

• Repeat the first turn again.
– Start with the MC on the left in your left hand
– Braid left over the middle with the MC
– Braid left over the middle again with the light solid
– Braid right over the middle with the plaid
– Braid left over the middle with the MC
– Braid left over the middle with the plaid
– Braid right over the middle with the light solid

• Braid 7 more loops counting them on the left edge

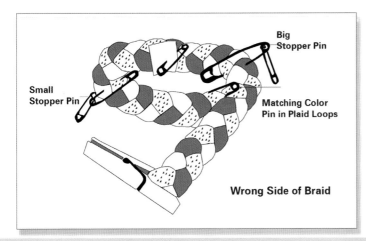

- Turn the braid over to the wrong side

- Use your 1st plaid as the MC

- Insert the *matching color pin*

- Place all the pins and make the snips the same way as when doing a regular butt.

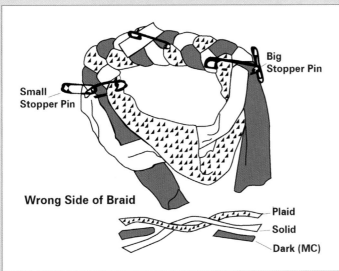

- Open the braid to the *stopper pins*

- Lay flat on the table with the wrong side up.

- To allow for braiding back the corners, you must cross your strips when sewing as shown

Tip: It is easier to re-braid if you do a blind stitch along the folded edges before braiding.

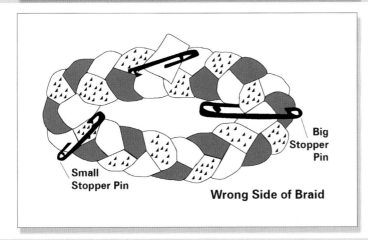

Be sure to start re-braiding at the *big stopper pin* end first. Make sure you rebraid so the corners are put back in the correct place.

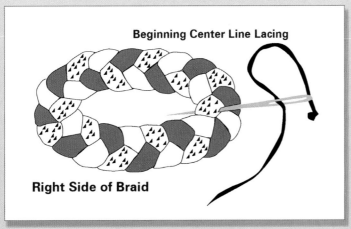

Lace this row using the Center Line Lacing Method (see *How to Lace*).

Practice Pattern: A 2 MC Basket

Use this small basket to practice the 2MC butt for the first row and regular butting for the remaining rows.

The Pattern

SR: No. of sets per row
INC: No. of increases
LBP: No. of loops between each pin
LME: No. of loops in the middle ends
LAL: Lace all loops
CLL: Center line lacing

2MC all-butted basket, made with double knit strips.

ROW	SR	INC	LBP	LME
1	2 MC	CLL		
2	10	5	0	0
3	12	3	2	0
4	16	6	1	1
5	16	LAL		
6	16	LAL		
7	16	LAL		
8	16	LAL		
9	16	LAL		
10	20	3 Loops between each pin		
11	20	LAL	Reverse Braid	

Handle = 7MC, Attach to top of basket and put 7 loops between handles

The bottom of the 2MC all-butted basket

LS   P   MC

Right Side of Braid

Row 1: Use the instructions for "Butting a 2-MC Oval Center, Row 1

All Other Rows: Place the fabric on the pin as in the normal way, and braid, butt and lace using the regular method. Remember to reverse braid the last row.

Place the MC (dark solid) strand on the pin first, followed by the plaid, and the light solid.

8 Loop Butted Center for Square Rugs

• Cut a piece of cardboard 2-1/2" X 3".

• Cut one strip of wool 1-1/4" X 17". Trim both ends on the right side by holding scissors straight across and point down toward you. If doing multiple squares, you can make one 17" strip for each of the squares that you are making.

• Fold the strip the same way as for regular braiding, from left to right, then over from right to left, then fold the entire strip in half.

• Either blind stitch the open edge or run a basting stitch the length of the strip, leaving 1" at each end free from stitching. You can braid, let the folds in place, and come back another time. Do not press the braid.

• The basted strip will be wrapped tightly around the cardboard, but don't stretch the wool. With the open seams to the left, leave 3/4" extra at the top of the cardboard and start wrapping from top to bottom on the side of the cardboard facing you, then coming up the back. Stop when the strip has wrapped around the front three times. Leave the excess at the end loose. Put a safety pin through the three folded strips on top, right to left, and close the pin.

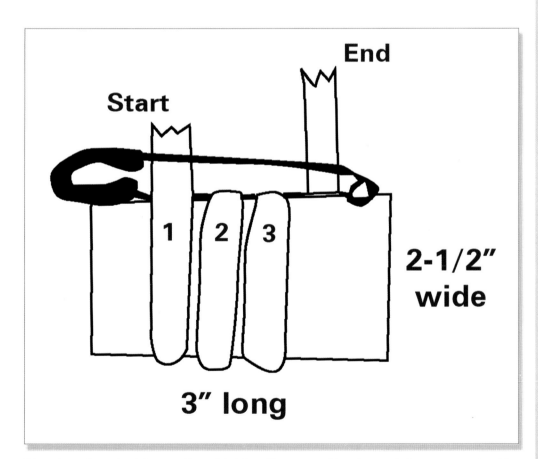

Wrap the strip around the cardboard tightly, without stretching the wool. Open seams should be to the left. Start at the top, leaving 3/4" above the cardboard, then come down the front and around to the back. Stop when there are three strands showing on the front of the card. Run a safety pin through the strip fabric on the top of the fold.

Right Side

The square rug center uses 1 strip, 1-1/4" x 17". With the right side facing up make a bias cut on the ends as shown. Fold the strip as usual, then either blind stitch the open edge or run a basting stitch the length of the strip. **Be sure to leave about an inch at each end open.**

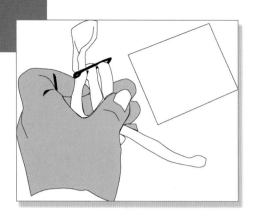

• Slide the folded strips off the cardboard.

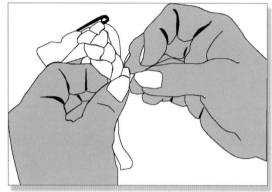

• At the pin, start braiding with the left over the middle.

Wrong Side of the Braid

Stitched Seam

• Continue until you have 8 loops, then sew ends together. Make sure to put right sides together then sew.

• Use needle nose pliers to even loops out.

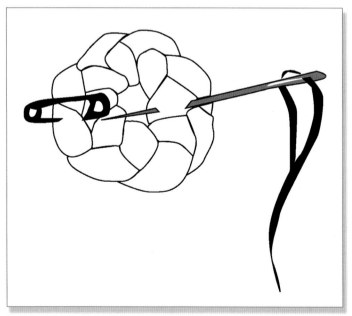

Lacing center of loop (see *How to Lace* for lacing instructions)

• Hide the knot going from the middle of the braid through the seam to the center of the loop just above the next loop.

• Lace all inside loops going 1-1/2 times around the center.

• To get the thread to outside of row, go underneath the loop that your lacing thread is sitting on top of going from left to right.

The 2nd row of a square has 2 loops in between each corner and those loops are the ones that are laced to the first 8-loop round.

4 corners X 2 loops = 8 loops = the 8 loop center.

9-Loop Butted Center for Round & Hexagon Rugs

• Cut 3 strips of wool 1-1/4" X 12", one of each of the colors that you are going to use

• Braid 5 sets

• Count 3 sets and pin MC-3 to MC-0 with the **matching color pin.** Don't forget to count your sets 0-1-2-3 and pin 3 to 0.

• Next place your **big stopper pin** one set to the right of your **matching color pin**, aiming the pin to the right and picking up ALL three colors. Close your pin.

• Now place the **small stopper pin** one set to the left of the **matching color pin**. This differs from a regular butt, where the *small stopper pin* is placed 2 sets to the left of the matching color pin. DO NOT CLOSE THE PIN.

• Place all your snipping pins as in the regular butt and make the snips.

• Carefully remove the small stopper pin (see drawing)

• With the pliers, pull the plaid loop toward the top of the braid making the plaid loop that you took the pin out of extra large.

Big Stopper Pin

Small Stopper Pin, Not Closed

Matching Color Pin

Wrong Side of Braid

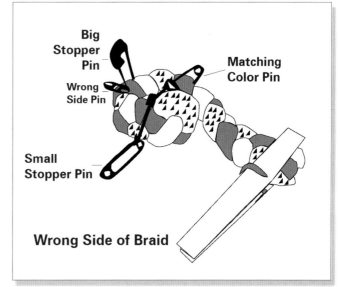

Big Stopper Pin

Wrong Side Pin

Matching Color Pin

Small Stopper Pin

Wrong Side of Braid

• Replace the small *stopper pin back* in the same two loops where it was.

• Place the **wrong side pin** and tag between the stopper pins. Use a piece of thread to hold the tag out of your way.

• Remove the *matching color pin* and the *beginning pin*. Cut on all the snips on both ends. Do not go up the 1/8" on the *small stopper pin* end, instead cutting through the snip like the cuts on the *big stopper pin* end.

• Sew the 2 outside strips together and blind stitch where the seams meet. Braid back starting with the *big stopper pin* end and sew the last middle strips, right sides together.

• Pull all the loops back into place.

• With the open folds to the outside, hide your knot and lace all the inside loops going around 1-1/2 times. Pull tight so that no hole shows in the middle when you are done.

Chapter 4

How To Lace

Lacing is the process of joining the braids into a rug. It is done with a special lacing thread that hides well between the loops and can be spliced together so there are no knots anywhere in the rug except at the very beginning. The lacing needle and thread go between the woolen loops, not through the fabric. When the lacing is complete, no thread will show and the fabric in the rug will not be weakened by being pierced. Be sure to use lacing thread #9, which has a tubular center and can be spliced together.

Before beginning to lace, some terms will be helpful to orient you.

Right side is the surface of your rug that will face the ceiling when the rug is done (though, in fact, our braided rugs are completely reversible). It is also the side of the braid that was facing you as you braided.

Right-hand side is the side or edge of the rug that is on your right side as you braid.

Rug side is the part of your rug you have already finished lacing; it is the center of your rug.

Braid side is the row or piece you are adding to the already-laced center or rug side.

Bottom row is the row that is closest to you when the rug is on a table, while you are lacing the center line or wherever you are lacing.

Top row is the row that is furthest away from you as you are lacing the center line.

Regular lacing means to lace every loop both on the rug side and the braid side.

Center Line Lacing

As the name implies, **Center Line Lacing** is used to lace the center of an oval or rectangular rug. Only Center Line Lacing is done on the right side of the rug; all other lacing is done on the wrong side. Lay your braid flat on the table in front of you with the right side of the braid facing up.

Thread the lacing needle and put a double knot in the lacing thread.

Lacing is done use #9 Lacing Thread. Thread the needle and place a double knot in the end.

Bring the needle through the seam of the inside middle plaid loop at the end where your first turn was made (**A** in the drawing). This is the only place in the rug where your needle actually pierces the fabric. You will notice this plaid loop and the light solid loop (**B** in the drawing), just above it and a little to the left, are the two loops used in making the corners and they are holding the corners together. These 2 loops will not be laced. We are only using the plaid loop to hide the knot.

The braid nearest you is the bottom row and the braid furthest away from you is the top row.

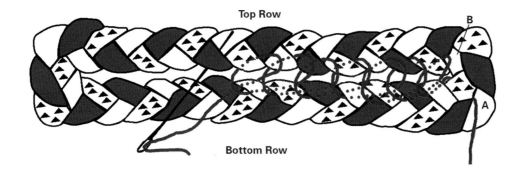

Top Row

Bottom Row

This drawing gives a basic overview of the stitching of the center line.

Bring the needle through the seam of the inside middle plaid loop at the end.

It comes out through the fold on the opposite side. This is the only place where the thread penetrates the fabric during lacing.

51

Start now by lacing:

- Bottom light solid (right to left)

- Top plaid (left to right)

- Back through the first bottom light solid again (right to left).

Remember to run the needle under a whole loop, not through any fabric. When going through the bottom loop the needle should be pointed down and to the left (8:00) and emerge in the middle of the loop. Then turn the needle up and to the right (2:00) to go through the upper loop.

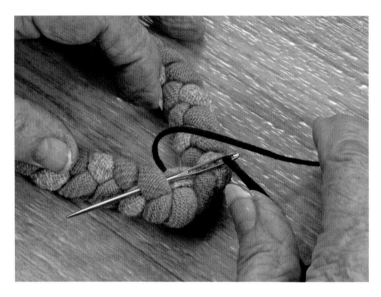

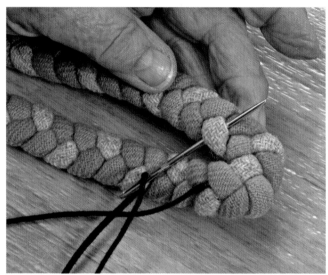

The remaining lacing goes behind the loop, not through the fabric. Continue on the bottom row, that is the row closest to you when the braid is on the table. Go through the bottom light solid, with the needle going right to left

Go through the top plaid loop with the needle going left to right

Then go back through the bottom light solid, right to left. Note that the thread goes through all the bottom loops twice and the top loops only once.

Tighten the thread so it snugly pulls the top and bottom together without distorting them.

When you've gone through the bottom light solid loop the second time, continue through the next bottom MC loop, which will be to the left. From there, go under the top MC and under the bottom MC again. You will notice you are lacing the bottom row loops twice and the top row loops only once.

After coming out of the light solid the second time, continue through the dark solid MC, again from right to left.

Then go through the MC on the top. In the center line, the Matching Colors (dark solids) match but the plaids and light solids do not. Through the rest of the rug, all the colors will match.

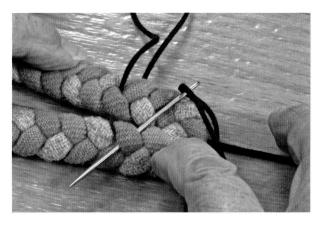

Come back through the MC in the bottom row...

Continue this way all along the center-line moving from right to left using the next loop to the left on the bottom row, the next loop on the top, and the already-laced loop on the bottom again. You will notice that every time you lace the matching color (MC) on the bottom, you will be lacing the matching color on the top. Light solid loops in the bottom row are laced to the plaid loops in the top row, and plaid loops in the bottom row are laced it to light solid loops on top. This "mismatch" occurs only in Center Line Lacing. Starting on the 2nd row, the colors of the two rows will match and you will be lacing each loop only once on the top and once on the bottom.

...and continue through the next bottom loop.

Continue along the Center Line in the same way.

The last 2 loops to be laced in the Center Line are a bottom plaid loop and a top light solid loop, then back through the bottom plaid loop.

Next you need to get the lacing thread to the outside edge of the row and on the wrong side of the rug ready to begin lacing the rest of your rug.

After going under that last bottom plaid for the 2nd time, go back through the top light solid loop aiming the needle to the right. Then go under the next loops on the top row, a matching color loop, a plaid loop and the next light solid loop. Your lacing thread is sitting on top of a plaid loop. Go under that loop aiming your needle to the left.

After going under that last bottom plaid for the 2nd time... ...go back through the top light solid loop aiming the needle to the right.

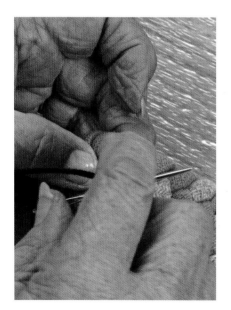

Go under the next loops on the top row, a matching color loop...

...a plaid loop...

...and the next light solid loop.

Your lacing thread is sitting on top of a plaid loop.

Go under that loop aiming your needle to the left.

Turn your rug over and notice that the lacing thread is now to the right of the MC.

Regular Lacing Steps

Now you are ready to start lacing on your 2nd row. Lace the matching color on the braid first, then lace a matching color on the rug. The matching color on the braid will fall slightly to the right of matching color on the rug.

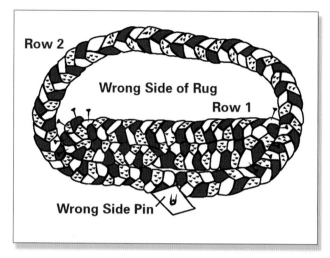

Regular lacing is done on the wrong side of the rug. Turn the rug over so the right side is facing down.

Lace under the MC loop on the braid side, that is the braid that you are adding.

With your right hand, pull the thread through towards the bottom left while holding the rug flat with your left hand.

Lace under the same color loop on the rug side.

Pull the thread towards the top left with your left hand while placing your right thumb under the braid you are adding to hold it up making the braid even with the rug and let the lacing thread pull the loop into position. **Always pull the lacing thread towards the left.**

How to Lace Increases

Increases are used to make turns in the rug. They are made by skipping one loop on the braid side. When the lacing needle is in the loop on the rug side that is just before the loop with the increase pin in it, skip the next loop on the braid side (not on the rug side) and lace the loop next to the one that you skipped then lace the loop that the pin is in on the rug side. Always do your skips on the braid side when increasing, never on the rug side, which would be a decrease. The only time you will skip on the rug side is when you are doing a special pattern such as making *Ruggies*™.

Pull the lacing thread just tight enough to hide the thread when doing your skips. If you pull too tight it will cause a bump.

The tag on the wrong side pin contains the information you need for making increases. It has the following information:

• The row number

• The total number of sets in the row (SR)

• The number of increases (INC)

• The number of loops between increase pins (LBP)

• The number of loops in the center of the row at each end (LME)

The rows marked "LAL" in the pattern have no increases and can be laced to the previous row away from the rug, and then put on following the increase instructions.

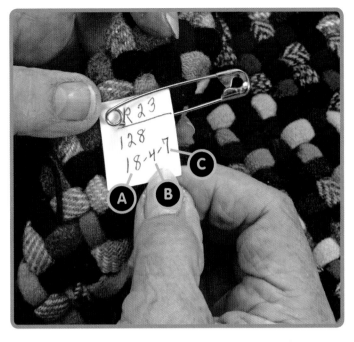

The information on the wrong side pin tag provides the lacing instructions. In this example we see that it is **Row 23** and that there are a total of **128 sets** in the row. The last line contains the increases. **A:** There are a total of 18 increases at each end. **B:** There are 4 empty-loops between the increase pins. **C:** There are 7 empty loops at the center of each end of the rug.

To find the center, align a thread with the center line of the first row and pull it to the edge of the rug.

This will show the center loop in the end of the rug.

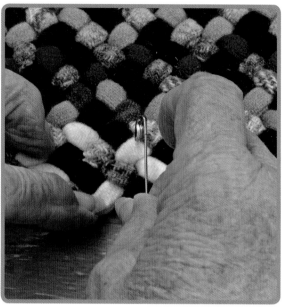

Place a safety pin in the center loop.

Refer to the wrong side pin tag. There are to be 7 loops in each end of the rug. This means three loops on each side of the center loop.

Count three loops to one side of the center loop and pin the fourth loop

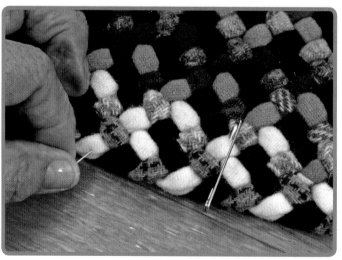

Count three empty loops to the other side of the center loop and pin the fourth.

Remove the safety pin from the center loop. There are now 7 empty loops between the two increase pins.

Moving away from the center, count four empty loops after the pin and place the next increase pin.

Repeat the process, 4 empty loops then a pin, until there are half of the increase pins called for in the pattern are on one side of the center. In this example that is 9 increase pins

Do the same on the other side of center and then repeat the steps at the other end. When you are finished there should be a total of 18 increase pins at each end, as called for in the pattern.

As you are lacing the braid to the rug and come to an increase pin, it is time to "skip school."

All increases are made in the braid, not the rug. Skip the loop that is opposite the increase pin...

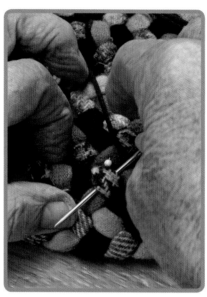

...and lace the next loop instead.

Go through the loop on the braid side...

...then lace the loop with the increase pin on the rug side.

Continue with the next loop on the braid side and make regular laces until you reach the next increase pin.

How to Lace Decreases

On some special designs, *Ruggies* for example, you will need to do a decrease. Decreases are made by skipping one loop on the rug side. When the lacing needle is in the loop on the rug side that is just before the loop with the decrease pin in it, skip the next loop on the rug side (not on the braid side) then lace the next loop on the braid side. Always do your skips on the rug side when decreasing, never on the braid side, which would be an increase. Pull your lacing thread a little tighter when doing your skips so your thread will not show.

The End of a Row

When you come to the end of a row, you need to get your lacing thread to the outside edge of the row before lacing on the next row. After the last lace, go under the loop your thread is sitting on, running your needle from left to right and bringing it through to the outside edge of the rug.

 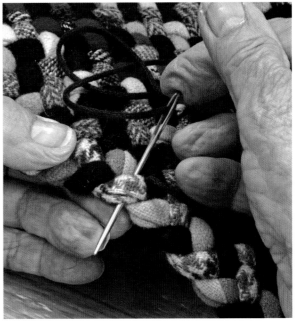

When you've laced the last loop in a row, continue for about 8 more loops. To get the thread to the outside, so you can begin the next row, make a last lace on the braid side. The thread will be over an outside loop.

Come through the outside loop, going from left to right.

Hold the next row in place so the Matching Color loops are aligned. Continue lacing. In this example, since the outside loop we last laced was a plaid, we begin lacing the next row with a plaid.

How to Splice Lacing Thread

When the thread is running out, a new piece is spliced onto the end. The directions that follow may make it sound much more complicated than it actually is. When you have spliced once or twice, you will find it quite simple. See Fig. 12x.

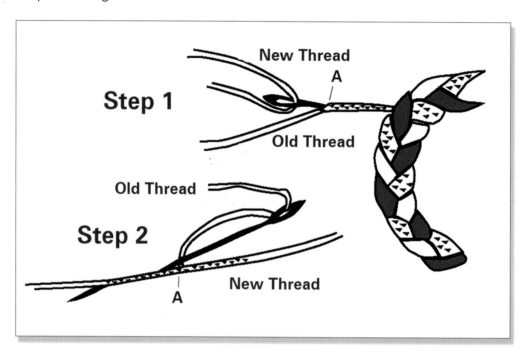

Add new thread to the old thread (I'm using white for this demonstration)

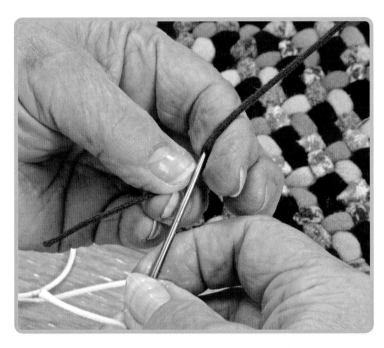

Slip the needle into the old thread about 3 inches from the end of the old thread and the rug (marked A in the drawing).

Run the needle down the center of the old thread until you get close to the rug...

...then bring the needle out the side of the old thread.

Pull the end of your new thread through the old...

...and take it off the needle.

Pull the new thread back into the old...

...so it doesn't show outside the old thread.

Step 2

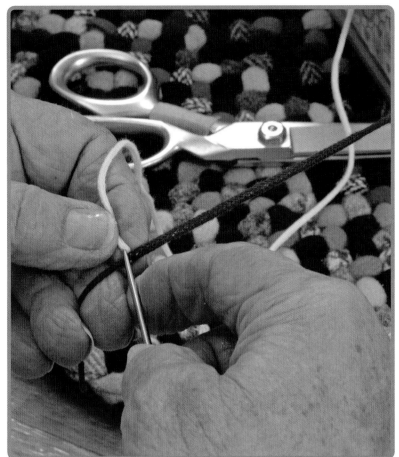

Insert the needle (unthreaded) into the new thread at the place where it entered the old thread. (A in the drawing on page 62)

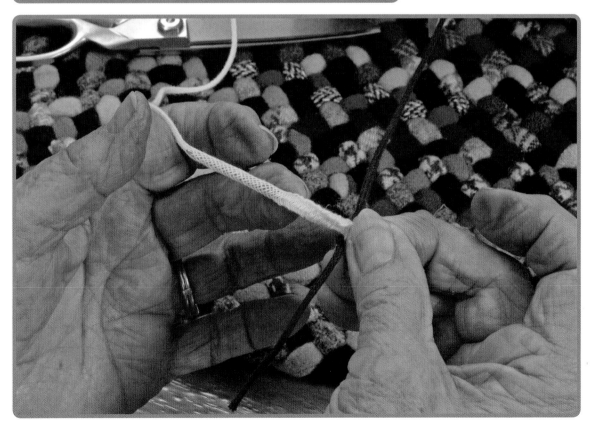

Slide the needle through the new thread for about the same distance as the loose tail of your old thread.

Bring the point of the needle out through the side of the new thread.

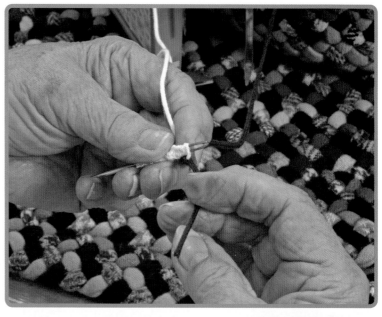

Thread the needle with the tail of the old thread...

...and slide the tube of the new thread over it...

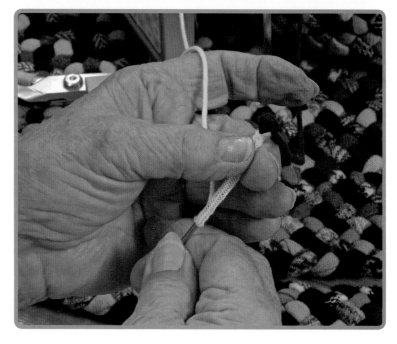

...pushing the new thread off the needle.

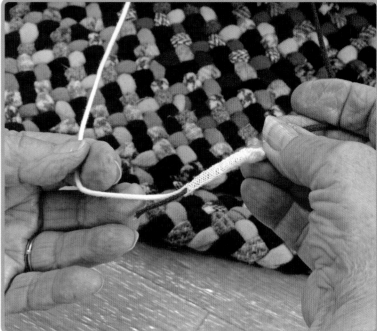

Take the needle off the old thread.

Pull on the new thread. The old thread will be tightly bound inside!

Chapter 5

Making an Oval
All-Butted Rug

The Pattern for a 2' X 3', 9MC Rug

SR: No. of sets per row
INC: No. of increases
LBP: No. of loops between each pin
LME: No. of loops in the middle ends
CLL: Center line lacing
LAL: Lace all loops

ROW	SR	INC	LBP	LME
1	9MC	CLL		
2	24	5	0	0
3	26	3	2	0
4	30	6	1	1
5	34	6	2	2
6	38	6	3	3
7	38	LAL		
8	44	9	2	0
9	44	LAL		
10	52	12	2	3
11	52	LAL		
12	52	LAL		
13	60	12	3	5
14	60	LAL		
15	60	LAL		
16	68	12	4	7
17	68	LAL		
18	68	LAL	Reverse Braid	

Braiding Row 1 of an Oval All-Butted Rug

• Braid 4 MCs according to your pattern

• Braid the first turn
- Start when the MC on the left in your left hand
- Braid left over the middle strand with the MC
- Braid left over the middle again with the light solid
- Braid right over the middle with the plaid
- Braid left over the middle with the MC
- Braid left over the middle with the plaid
- Braid right over the middle with the light solid.

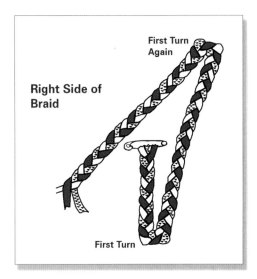

Right Side of Braid

First Turn Again

First Turn

• Continue braiding 9 matching colors counting on the inside of the braid, then repeat the first turn.
- Start the turn when the MC on the left in your left hand
- Braid left over the middle with the MC
- Braid left over the middle again with the light solid
- Braid right over the middle with the plaid
- Braid left over the middle with the MC
- Braid left over the middle with the plaid
- Braid right over the middle with the light solid

• Braid the 5 MCs plus an additional 2 sets. Butt this row together.

Braiding Rows 2-19

Braid and butt all the other rows following the pattern for the number of sets in each row and the planning sheet for the order that the colors are placed on the pin.

Remember:

• Add two additional sets to give you enough to do your butting.

• Pin each row with the wrong side tag

• Reverse braid for the last row.

When the rows are all braided it is time to lace the rows together, following the Center Line Lacing and the increasing instructions.

Chapter 6

Spiral Method

The spiral method is probably one of the original methods used for braiding rugs. Although the butted method is now the braiding technique I prefer, some still like to use the spiral method.

Spiral braiding uses one continuous braid for the rug, instead of the many concentric rows in an all-butt rug. The last row can be butted to soften the tapered end and to introduce the beginner to The Perfect Butt™ method for butting rows together. The oval spiral also teaches the beginner's hands to braid and lace, and to develop a standard size of braid.

Preparing the Enclosed End

• Cut 3 strips of fabric 1-1/2" wide

• Fold the material as you did for the butt strips, but fold the right sides together and stitch from the folded edge, making a right angle as shown by the dotted lines in the (Drawing: A & B).

• Trim the corner in 2 directions, as shown. (Drawing: A & C).

• Turn the folded strip right side out. Do this for all three strips. (Drawing: D).

• Hand sew the three strips together, side by side. Do not stitch tightly and do not overlap. (Drawing: E & F).

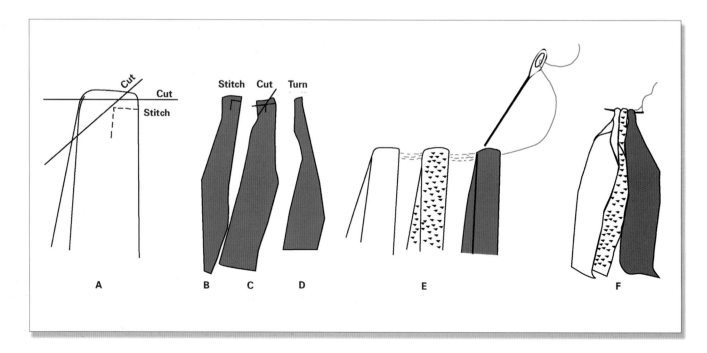

Turns for the First Spiral Row

First Turn

• Braid the number of MCs according to the size you have chosen

• Braid the first turn
  – Start With the MC on the left in your left hand
  – Braid left over the middle with the MC
  – Braid left over the middle again with the light solid
  – Braid right over the middle with the plaid
  – Braid left over the middle with the MC
  – Braid left over the middle with the plaid
  – Braid right over the middle with the light solid.

• Continue braiding the total number of sets (MC) according to the size you have chosen.

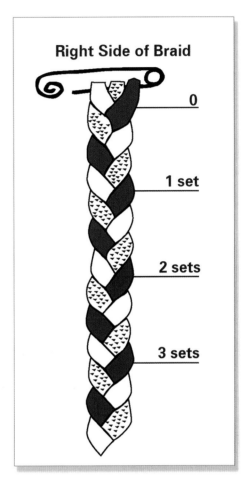

Right Side of Braid

0

1 set

2 sets

3 sets

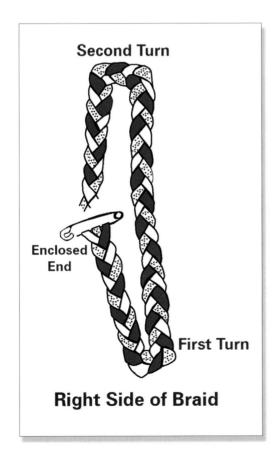

Second Turn

Enclosed
End

First Turn

Right Side of Braid

Braiding the Oval Spiral

Place the strips on a safety pin, with the Light Solid (LS) on the left.

• Braid left (LS) over the middle

• Braid right (MC) over the middle

• Braid left (PL) over the middle

• Braid right (LS) over the middle

Reminder: Whenever you want to stop braiding, place a clothespin over your last completed braid to hold it in place until you are ready to start again.

Braid the number of sets for the center you need for the rug size you are making. When counting sets, it is very important that your first MC loop be counted as 0 (zero). When you have the correct number of sets, you will be ready for the 1st turn.

- Braid the Second Turn
  - Start with the LS on the left in your left hand
  - Braid left over the middle with the LS
  - Braid left over the middle again with the PL
  - Braid right over the middle with the MC
  - Braid left over the middle with the LS
  - Braid right over the middle with the PL
  - Braid left over the middle with the MC
  - Braid left over the middle with the plaid
  - Braid right over the middle with the light solid

- When you are ready to lace, the pin end will be sewn into the second turn.

- Continue braiding and lacing the regular way until you are ready for a color change.

Color Change In Oval Rug

Place the rug on the table with the wrong side up and the enclosed end nearest your left hand and the first turn end nearest your right hand. Put a safety pin on the top left hand curve. This is the color change curve. Make sure you have made all the increases and braided about 2"of braid beyond the curve.

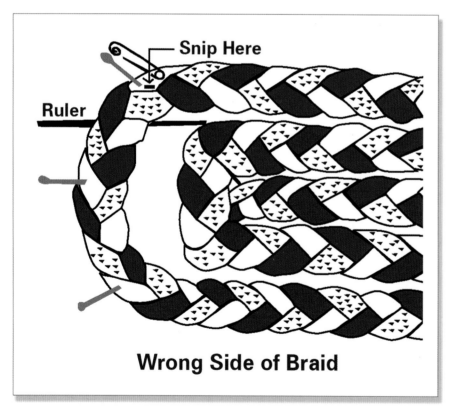

Snip Here

Ruler

Wrong Side of Braid

Place a ruler along the straight edge of the rug. Put a finger on the last outside loop (of the color you are changing) nearest the curve. This is the loop you will snip and change the color. This now leaves the old color nearest the rug and the new color away. Snip this loop just before it goes under the next loop. Unbraid it and trim at the slight angle just above the snip. Hold the right side of wool up and the braided end away from you and point the handles of the scissors up and the points down. Trim the new color the same way with the roll away from you and join them with 1/4" seam, placing right sides together. When you rebraid, this seam will fall under another loop and will not show on either side.

Keep the color changes just after the curve and just before the straight edge. Don't ever make a color change on the straight side. Continue braiding up to the next to the last row and taper off at the end of this row.

Tapering is always done on a curve.

• Braid up to the curve and cut the braid straight across about where the safety pin is shown in the drawing for the color change.

• Lace only to 7" before the curve

• Unbraid and open up each strand of wool and fold it in half with the folded edge to the left and the open edge to the right.

• Starting at the bottom, cut the open edges off from nothing up to the regular size.

• End up in three different places to the regular size, the first about 1/2" from the lacing, the second about 1-1/2" from the lacing, and the third one about 2" from the lacing.

• Refold the braid and sew with a blind stitch to hold it in place.

• Re-braid down to the end. The ends will be uneven, but this is what you want.

• Sew end 1 to end 2 and end 2 to end 3

• Lace the taper to the rug, increasing as little as possible. Run the lacing thread to the row before the tapered row and re-lace about seven loops. Then bring the lacing thread to the outside of the row ready to lace on the last butted row.

• The last butted row you braid with your open seams to the right and butt using The Perfect Butt™ method.

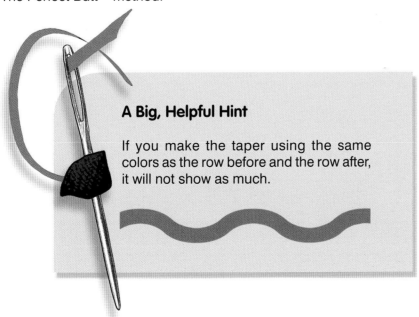

A Big, Helpful Hint

If you make the taper using the same colors as the row before and the row after, it will not show as much.

How to Lace a Spiral Rug

Lacing the Spiral First Round

• Lace on the right side of the rug for center line lacing and completing the enclosed end.

• Lace on the wrong side for completing the rest of the rug

Lay your braid flat on a table in front of you with the right side of the braid facing up. Remember the right side of the braid is the side that was facing you when you braided. Lacing is done on the right side of the rug only for the center line lacing. All the rest of the lacing is done on the wrong side of the rug. The enclosed end (second turn) should be nearest your left hand and the first turn end will be nearest your right hand.

Center Line Lacing (CLL) for an Oval Spiral

Thread the lacing needle and put a double knot in the lacing thread. The double knot is necessary so it won't pull through the material. Bring the needle through the seam of the inside middle plaid loop on the end where the first turn was made. Except for the enclosed end, this is the only other place in the rug where the needle actually pierces the fabric. You will notice that this plaid loop and the light solid loop just above it and a little toward the left are the two loops used in making the corners and they hold the corners together. These 2 loops will NOT be laced. We only use the plaid loop to hide the knot in.

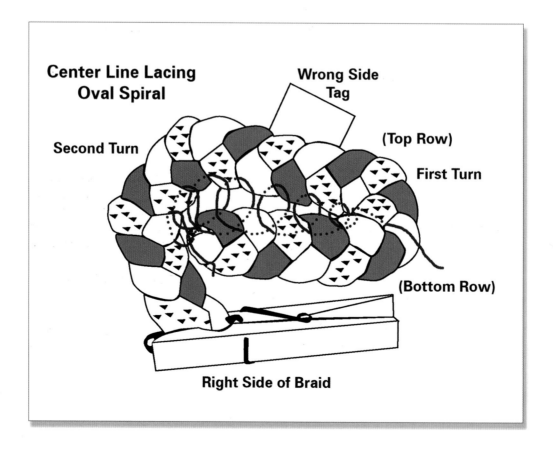

Center Line Lacing Oval Spiral

Wrong Side Tag

Second Turn

(Top Row)

First Turn

(Bottom Row)

Right Side of Braid

The braid nearest you is the bottom row and the braid furthest away from you is the top row. Start now by lacing:

Bottom light solid (right to left)
Top plaid (left to right)
Lace back through the first bottom light solid again (right to left).

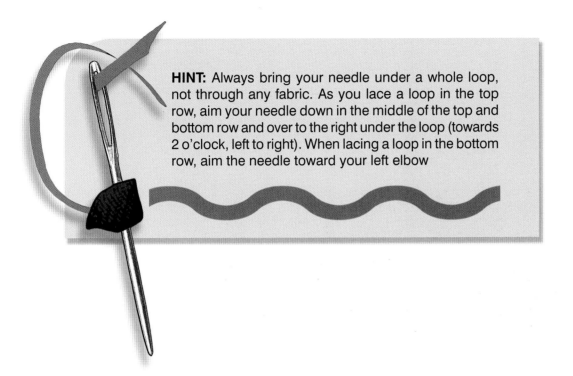

HINT: Always bring your needle under a whole loop, not through any fabric. As you lace a loop in the top row, aim your needle down in the middle of the top and bottom row and over to the right under the loop (towards 2 o'clock, left to right). When lacing a loop in the bottom row, aim the needle toward your left elbow

Now, bring the needle under the next bottom MC to the left of the one you just did and lace:

• Bottom MC (right to left)

• Top MC (left to right)

• Lace through the first bottom MC again (right to left).

Continue this way all along the center line using the next loop on the left in the bottom row, and the next loop on the top, then the already-laced loop on the bottom again. You will notice that a matching color loop on the bottom will be laced to a matching color loop on the top row, a light solid loop in the bottom row will be laced it to a plaid loop in the top row, and a plaid loop in the bottom row will be laced to a light solid loop on top. This "mismatch" occurs only in center line lacing. When lacing on the 2nd row, all the loop colors will match each other and you will be lacing each loop only once on the top and once on the bottom.

When you come to the last 2 loops at the end of the row of the center line lacing, you will be lacing a bottom light solid loop, then top plaid loop, then the bottom light solid loop again. This is the end of the center line lacing.

How to Lace Around the Enclosed End (the Second Turn End) of an Oval Spiral Rug

Work on the right side of the rug.

• Insert the needle through the back side of the material at the base of the MC loop on the enclosed end, right to left. Come out in the left corner at the top between the MC and the plaid loop.

• Lace under the whole MC loop on the braid side, left to right.

• Sew back through the seam of this MC loop, keeping to the left of the loop.

• Sew through the MC tip on the enclosed end, right to left.

• Sew through the tip end of the plaid on the enclosed end, right to left

• Lace the plaid loop on the rug side.

• Lace the MC loop on the braid side.

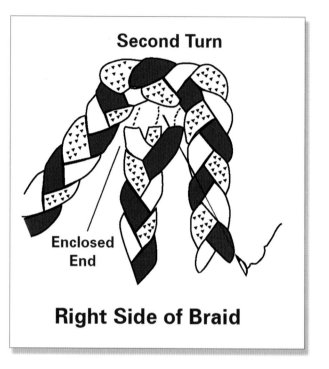

Second Turn

Enclosed End

Right Side of Braid

• Lace the MC loop on the rug side.

• Lace under whole plaid loop on braid side, left to right.

• Sew back through the seam of the same plaid loop end keeping to the left of the loop.

• Sew again through the tip middle plaid on the enclosed end, right to left.

• Sew through the tip end of light solid, right to left on the enclosed end.

• Lace under light solid on the braid side, left to right.

• Sew back through the seam of this same loop keeping to the left of the loop.

• Sew through the light solid tip on the enclosed end again, right to left.

Turn the rug over to the wrong side, and regular lace the plaid loop on the braid side. **Note:** The MC on the braid side should always fall just to the right of the MC on the rug side.

Row 2

Do regular lacing now on this wrong side to the other end, lacing one loop on the braid side and one loop on the rug side. At this first end (First Turn) put in 5 increase pins as shown.

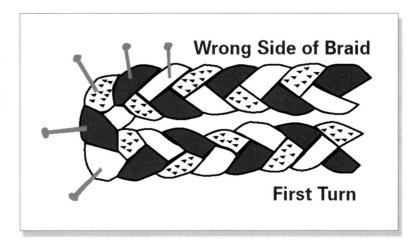

At the next end (Second Turn) put in 6 increase pins as shown.

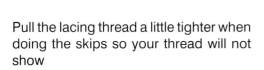

Pull the lacing thread a little tighter when doing the skips so your thread will not show

This completes your Row 2.

Follow your Oval Spiral Mat Pattern to know where and how many increases to make to finish the remaining rows

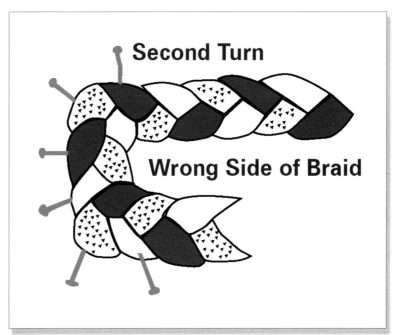

Last Row:

Lace the taper to the rug increasing as little as possible. Next, run lacing thread to the row before the tapered row, re-lace about seven loops, and cut off the end of the lacing thread.

Note: When making a larger spiral rug, the last row is always butted using The Perfect Butt™ method and braiding with the open seams to the right instead of the left so no seams show in the complete rug. The butted row gives a nice smooth shape to your rug and hides the taper.

Spiral Oval Rug Pattern

Here is a 2' x 3' rug pattern for a small spiral rug

INC: No. of increases
LBP: No of loops between each pin
LME: No. of loops in the middle ends
LAL: Lace all loops
CLL: Center line lacing

ROW	INC	LBP	LME
1	CLL		
2*	5	0	0
	6	0	0
3	3	2	0
4	6	1	1
5	6	2	2
6	6	3	3
7	LAL		
8	9	2	0
9	LAL		
10	12	2	3
11	LAL		
12	LAL		
13	12	3	5
14	LAL		
15	LAL		
16	12	4	7
17	LAL		
18	LAL	Reverse Braid	

Note: the count for row 2 is different on each side.

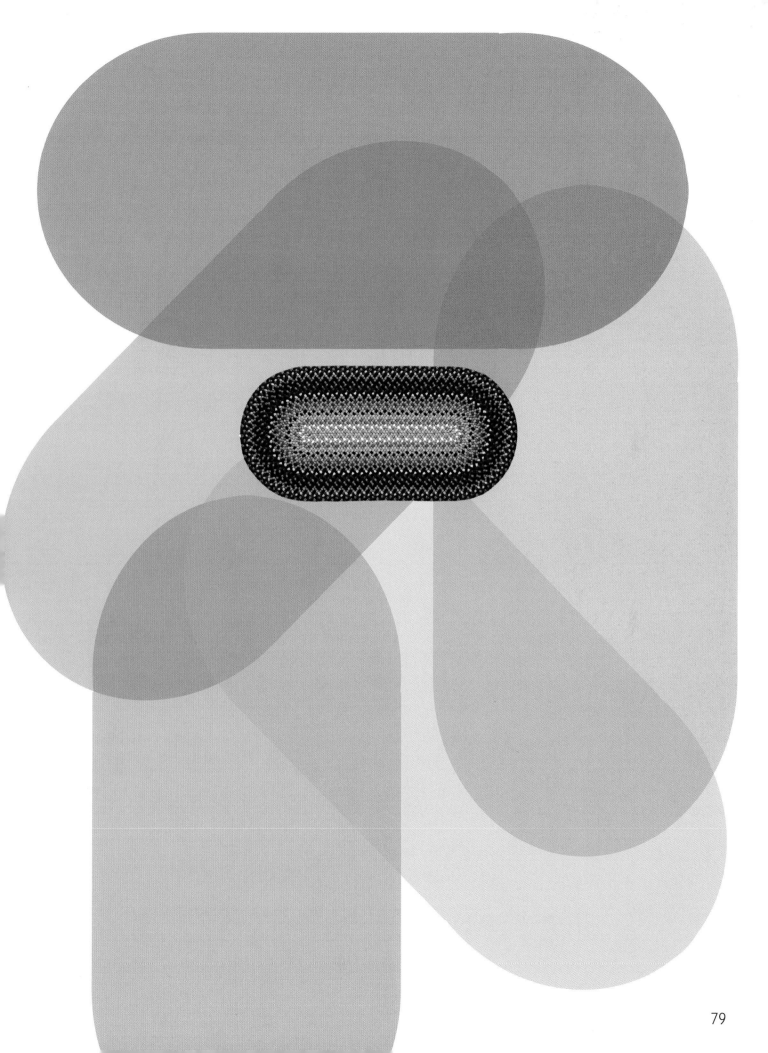

Chapter 7

Let's Make a Pair of Ruggies™

Where Ruggies™ Were Born

Ruggies™ were named at one of many family gatherings at our cottage on Lake Sunapee in New Hampshire. As always Barbara was having fun with her braiding and tried her hand at making slippers for her children and grandchildren. They decided that they were more than slippers and after much debate they came to be named Ruggies™. From that day forward our Ruggies™ have been worn everywhere, from home lounging to college dormitories.

May the Ruggies that you make bring you the joy and comfort that they have brought to our family for many years.

Ruggies™ Sizing & Patterns

Sizing for Ruggies™ is not as exact as a pair of shoes would be. It is a trial-and-error process and a lot depends upon the width and weight of the wool you use, how loosely or tightly you braid, and the pattern you choose. The most common size that I make is a 5MC. If you make this size first, you can use it to determine the rest of your sizing range. The difference between a 4MC and 5MC is not one shoe size.

To help you estimate the Ruggies size, here is a chart that gives a rough comparison to standard footwear sizes.

Ruggies Size	Child's Size	Women's Size	Men's Size
3MC	BabyRuggies	4	-
4MC	7	5 to 6	8
5MC	8-1/2	7 to 8	8 to 9-1/2
6MC	–	9 to 10	10 to 12

A new pair of Ruggies™ will feel weird at first, but the soft wool fabric will eventually conform to your feet. When you first wear the Ruggies, mark the one on your right foot in some way and always put that one on your right foot. As it takes the shape of your foot, you won't need the marker.

Ruggies™ can be washed with on the delicate cycle, using cold water and a pinch of Woolite. Do not put them in the dryer. Warning: the pompoms will get messed up in the washer.

The bottoms of the Ruggies will wear out faster than the tops if they don't have leather bottoms attached. The bottoms can be replaced, but there is no guarantee that you will still have the same fabric as the top when the time comes.

Ruggies™ are good projects for advanced braiders and are made using only the all-butted method.

Patterns

SR: Number of sets per row
INC: Increase
LBP: Number of loops between each pin
LAL: Lace all loops
LME: Number of loops in the middle ends
CLL: Center line lacing
REV: Reverse the seams
DEC: Decrease

• When using only 7 rows in an 8 row pattern, use rows 1, 2 & 3 for the bottom, eliminate row 4, and use rows 5, 6, 7 & 8 for the top.

• All last rows have a total of 8 decreases: 5 in the toe end and 3 in the heel end.

Refer to page 16, row 8.

• 3MC

ROW	SR	INC	LBP
Bottom			
1	3MC	CLL	–
2	12	5 INC	0
3	14	3 INC	2
Top			
4	14	LAL	–
5	13	3-Dec	2
6	11	6-Dec	1
7	9 REV	5-Dec	1

• 4MC

ROW	SR	INC	LBP
Bottom			
1	4MC	CLL	–
2	14	5 INC	0
3	16	3 INC	2
Top			
4	16	LAL	–
5	15	3-Dec	2
6	13	6-Dec	1
7	11 REV	5-Dec	1

• 5MC

ROW	SR	INC	LBP
Bottom			
1	5MC	CLL	–
2	16	5 INC	0
3	18	3 INC	2
4	18	LAL	–
Top			
5	18	LAL	–
6	17	3-Dec	2
7	15	6-Dec	1
8	13 REV	5-Dec	1

• 6MC

ROW	SR	INC	LBP
Bottom			
1	6MC	CLL	–
2	18	5INC	0
3	20	3 INC	2
4	20	LAL	–
Top			
5	20	LAL	–
6	19	3-Dec	2
7	17	6-Dec	1
8	15 REV	6-Dec	1

SMALL BRAID

• 3MC			
ROW	**SR**	**INC**	**LBP**
Bottom			
1	3MC	CLL	–
2	12	5 INC	0
3	12	LAL	–
Top			
4	12	LAL	–
5	10	6-Dec	1
6	8 REV	5-Dec	1

• 4MC			
ROW	**SR**	**INC**	**LBP**
Bottom			
1	4MC	CLL	–
2	14	5 INC	0
3	14	LAL	–
Top			
4	14	LAL	–
5	13	3-Dec	2
6	11	6-Dec	1
7	9 REV	5-Dec	1

TINY BRAID

• 2MC			
ROW	**SR**	**INC**	**LBP**
Bottom			
1	2MC	CLL	–
2	10	5 INC	0
Top			
3	10	LAL	–
4	9	3-Dec	2
5	8 REV	5-Dec	1

Refer to the pattern you have chosen to determine how many matching colors (MC) to put in the center.

In making Ruggies, matching the colors is imperative, so it is easier if you use 3 different colors, a light solid, a plaid and a dark solid. The dark solid will be called the MC. You can carry the same MC throughout your Ruggies.

You need approximately 1-1/2 yards of wool cut in widths of 1-1/2" for each pair. Remember the weight and width of the wool strips greatly affects the size of your Ruggies. Narrower wool makes smaller, narrower Ruggies, and wider wool makes larger, wider Ruggies (see illustration on page 18).

Place the strips of wool on the pin the regular way, and start braiding the left light solid over the middle plaid first. Keep your open edges to the left.

When you have half the number of MCs needed for the center, braid the first turn. Starting with the MC, braid MC left-left-right then left-left-right again.

Continue by braiding the number of sets called for in the pattern then repeat the first turn. Make sure you start each turn with the MC. Continue braiding again until you overlap the beginning of your braid.

Now braid all but the last row, butting them in regular rings with no turns.

The Last Row

The last row is always braided reversing the open edges. That means to braid with the open edges to the right instead of the left as in the other rows.

Again place the wool strips on the pin the regular way and start braiding the left light solid over the middle plaid first.

Braid five MC sets, counting on the right hand side. Make a corner starting with the MC in your right hand and braid MC right-right-left then right-right-left again. Continue braiding until you have the final count.

The count will look different. You must count your MCs on the right hand side.

When butting this last row, snip both folded edges and when cutting on the snips aim the scissors away (upward) instead of toward (downward) as it is done in regular butting.

Bottom of Ruggies

Row 1: Lay the braid flat on the table in front of you with the right side of the braid facing up. (The right side of the braid is the side that was facing you when you braided it.) For an illustrated guide to lacing the center line, see Center Line Lacing, page 50 and following.

Thread the lacing needle with lacing thread #9 and put a double knot in one end. You need a double knot so it won't pull through the material. Bring the needle through the seam of the inside middle plaid loop on the end where the first turn was made. (There are only two places in the Ruggies where your needle actually pierces the fabric; this is the first.) You will notice this plaid loop and the light solid loop just above it and a little toward the left are the two loops used in making the corners and they are holding the corners together. These two loops will not be laced. We are only using the plaid loop to hide the knot.

The braid nearest you is the bottom row and the braid furthest away from you is the top row. Start now by lacing:

- the bottom light solid (right to left)
- then the top plaid (left to right)
- then back through the first bottom light solid again (right to left).

Remember to bring your needle under a whole loop, not through any fabric. In doing this lacing, as you lace a loop in the top row, aim your needle down in the middle of the top and bottom row and up to the right under the loop (towards two o'clock) like you are thumbing a ride. When lacing a loop in the bottom row, aim the needle toward your left elbow (towards eight o'clock).

Continue this way all along the center line using the next loop on the left in the bottom row, and the next loop on the top, then the already-laced loop on the bottom again. You will notice you are lacing the bottom row loops twice and the top row loops only once.

Every time you lace your matching color on the bottom, you will be lacing your matching color on the top. When you are lacing your light solid in the bottom row, you will be lacing it to your plaid in the top row, and when you are lacing your plaid in the bottom row, you will be lacing it to your light solid in the top row. This "mismatch" occurs only in center line lacing. When lacing on your second row, all your colors will match each other and you will be lacing each loop only once on the top and once on the bottom.

When you come to the end of the row with your center line lacing, the last two loops you will be lacing will be a bottom plaid loop, then top light solid loop, then the bottom plaid loop again. This is the end of the center line lacing.

Now we have to get the lacing thread to the outside edge of the row. To do this, after going under that last bottom plaid, you now will notice your lacing thread is on the top of the matching color loop in the bottom loop of the bottom row.

Lace underneath this matching color loop. Now your lacing thread is in between your MC loop and your light solid loop ready to start lacing on your second row. Continue working on the right side of your Ruggies.

Row 2: Match up your pattern by putting the MC of the second row to the right of the MC on the first row. Lace your MC on the braid then go back to lace your MC on the first row. Now do five skips on each end by placing five pins in each loop starting with the first loop of the corner on the right side of the Ruggie™ which will be the plaid loop.

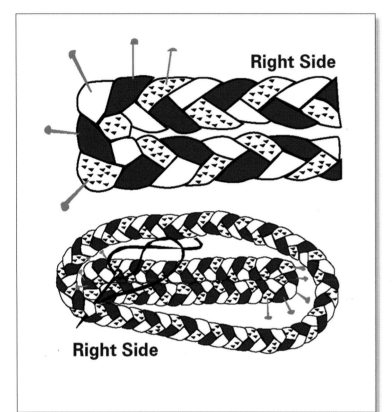

Right Side

Right Side

Your first pin is now in the plaid loop just to the left of your matching color. This means when your lacing needle is in a loop just before a loop that has a pin in it, the lacing needle says to the pin, "let's skip school across the street", meaning that you skip the next loop on the braid side then go back and lace the loop with the pin in it. Do this until you have skipped all five times. If this is done correctly, your MCs on the braid side will fall just to the right of your MC in the first rows.

Row 3: Match up your pattern by putting the MC in the third row to the right of the MC in row two. Then do three skips in the plaid loops on each end leaving one pin in the middle of the end and two loops between the pins going down the sides.

Row 4: Match up your colors by putting the MC on row four to the right of the MC on row three, then lace all loops. This row will start to curl towards the wrong side to form the sole of the Ruggies.

You have now completed the bottom of your Ruggies. Put this aside until the top is completed. (Note: When using only 7 rows, skip row 4).

Top of Ruggies™

Rows 5 & 6: On the right side of the braid, match up the colors by putting the MC from the braid of row 6 to the right of the MC from row five on the Ruggies side.

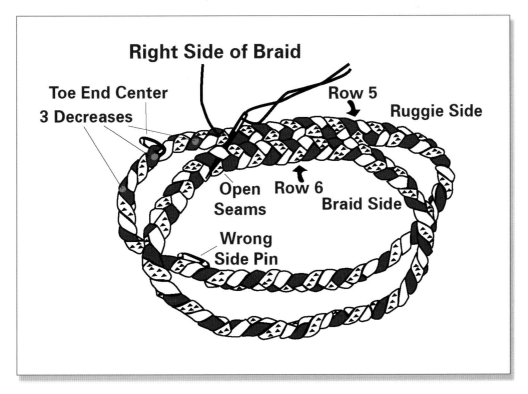

Put a double knot in one end of your lacing thread.

In row 5, insert the lacing needle in between the seam of the MC loop and pierce the fabric to hide the knot.

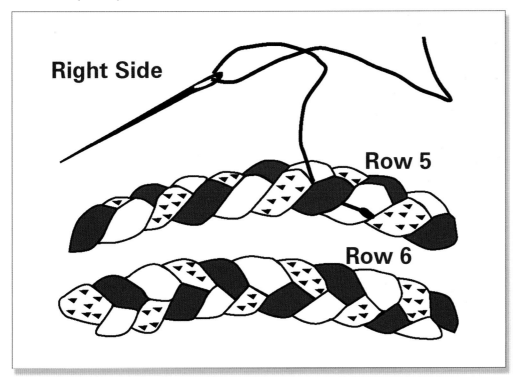

Next, lace the plaid loop to the left still on row 5.

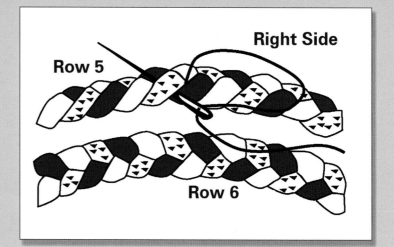

Now lace the light solid loop in row 6.

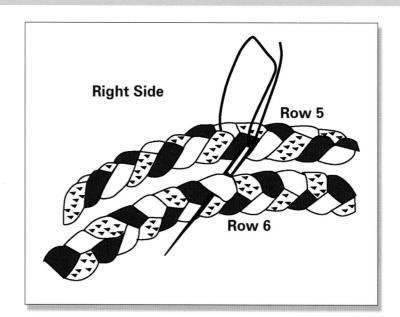

Continue lacing for at least three MC sets before starting to do the decreases.

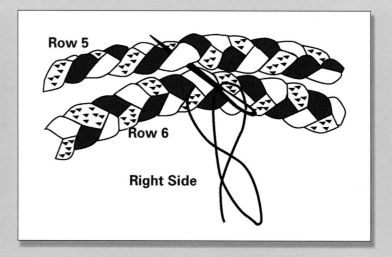

On the toe end, make three decreases on row 5. They must be three MCs that you decrease on the Ruggies side, which is row 5. The middle MC that you decreased on is the center of the toe end. Mark with a large safety pin. Then finish lacing every loop for the rest of the row.

Row 7: Find the middle of row six, which is a plaid loop in line with the MC center of row 5 that you have marked with a large safety pin. Now extend the large safety pin into the center plaid loop to keep a mark on the center of the toe end

Do six decreases on just the toe end. Hold the top of the Ruggies with the toe end is pointed away from you.

Moving to the right from the center plaid loop, mark your decreases from the center plaid loop by:

- placing a pin in the first loop to the right
- skipping a loop
- placing a pin in the next loop
- skipping a loop
- placing a pin in the next loop.

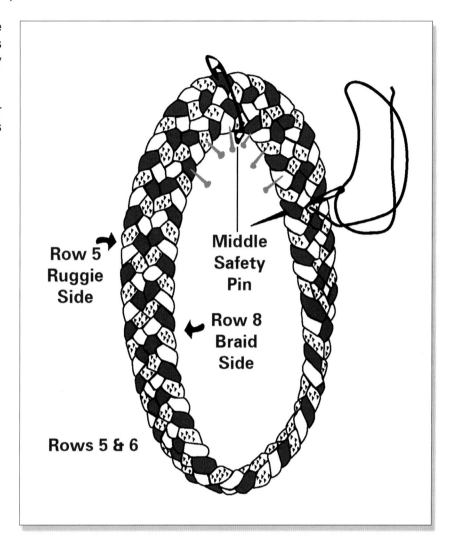

This makes a total of three pins to the right of center in row 7, which mark your decreases.

Go back to the center plaid loop and work to the left to mark your remaining decreases by:

- placing a pin in the first loop to the left
- skipping a loop
- placing a pin in the next loop
- skipping a loop
- placing a pin in the next loop.

This gives a three decrease pins to the left.

Now you have a total of six pins marking the six decreases. Finish lacing every loop for the rest of the row. Remember decreases are when you skip on the Ruggies side not the braid side.

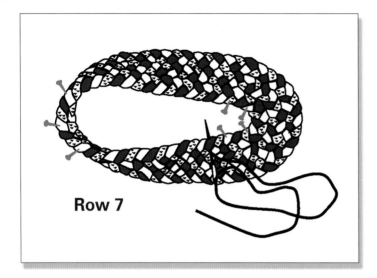

Row 7

Row 8: Don't match up your colors when lacing row eight to row seven. Put your plaid loop in the middle of the plaid loops on row 7 and make five decreases on the toe end.

Find the middle of row 8, which will be a MC. Mark that MC to skip then mark two skips on each side with one loop in between each skip.

On the heel end, make three decreases in the light solid loops. Mark the decreases by placing a pin in the middle light solid. Mark each light solid loop on each side to skip and finish lacing the row. Lace all the way down to the end of the toe end opening.

Lace up the middle of this last row only to 1 loop before where the second set of MC's meet using the center line lacing method. Lace backwards to end off your lacing thread. Do not use this lacing thread to attach the pompom.

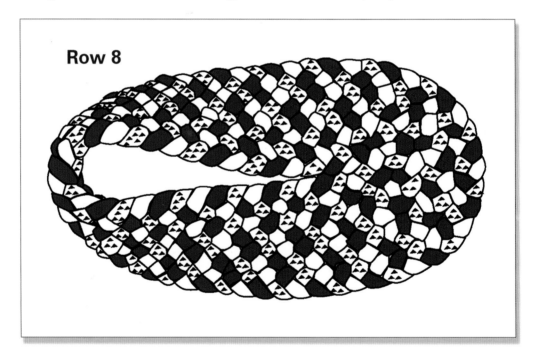

Row 8

Finishing: Join the top of the Ruggie™ to the bottom by putting the plaid loop of one row in the middle of the 2 plaid loops of the otehr row (or light solids in the middle of the light solids) and lacing all the loops.

Pompoms: Cut three 36-inch strips of wool of the same colors you used in your Ruggies™ into 1/8-inch widths. Cut into five-inch lengths, divide in half and tie each group together with a new piece of lacing thread. Attach a pompom to each Ruggie™ with the lacing thread used to tie the pompom.

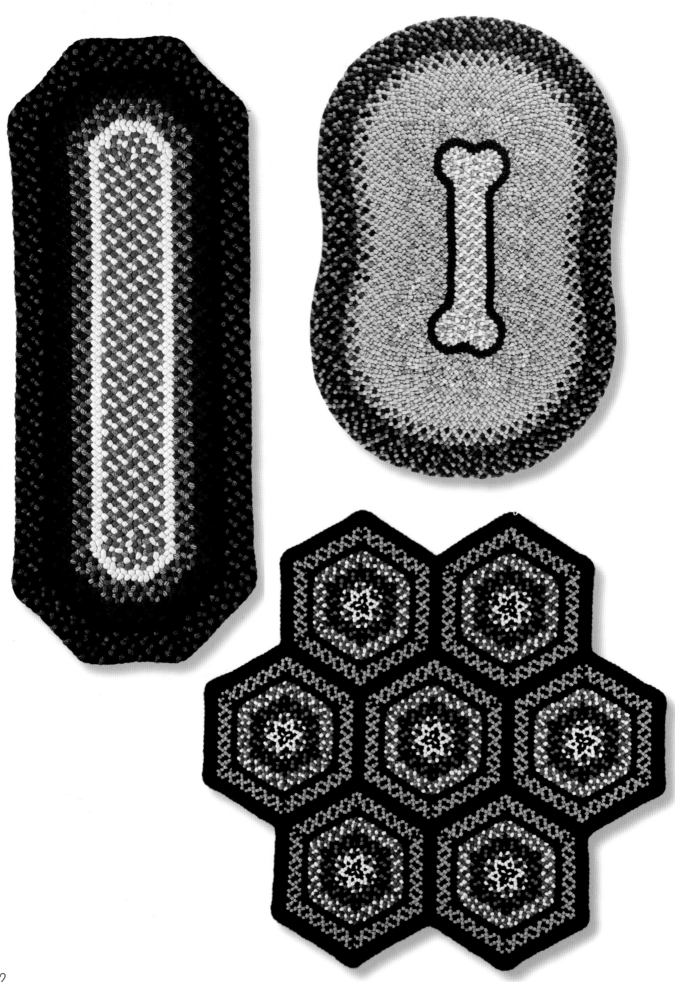

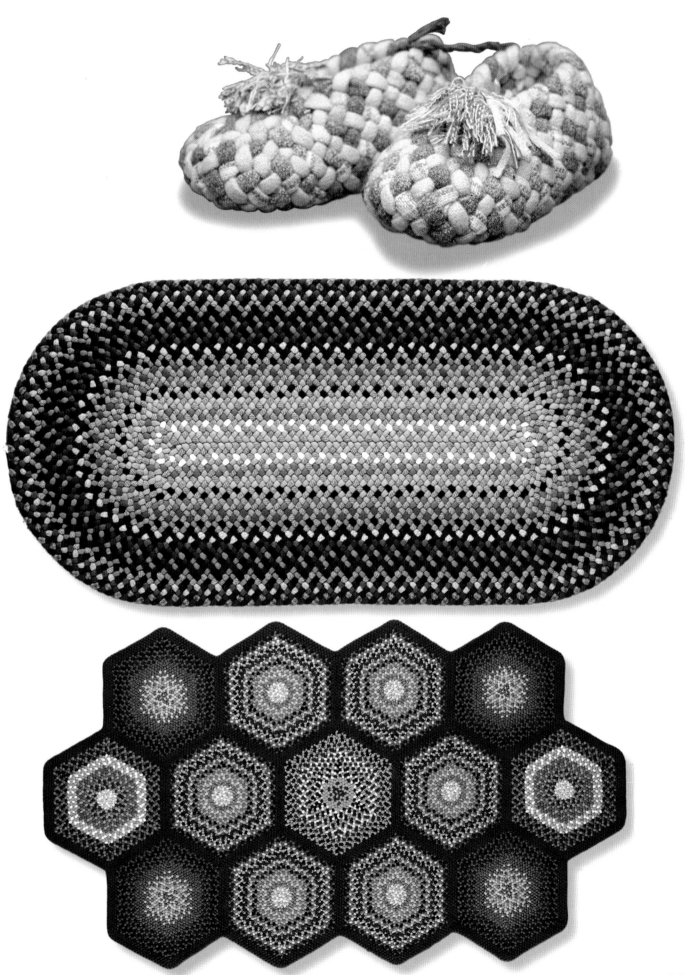

Glossary of Terms

butting. Method of joining the beginning of a row to the end so that it forms a complete circle

center line. The line formed when the first row is laced

dark solid. The darkest solid in the braid

decrease. Taking away a loop on the rug side

enclosed end. Finishing the beginning or end of a row

first turn. LLR, LLR

hit-or-miss rug. Braided with small strips of wool of various colors randomly scattered throughout the rug

increase. Adding an extra loop on the braid side

lacing. Attaching the new braid to the body of the rug

light solid. The lightest solid in the braid

loop. One of the three tubes after it has been braided.

matching color (MC). The darkest, most prominent color, put on the pin first and used for counting sets

modified corner. Left-left-right

plaid. A geometrical pattern, the term is used here to denote any patterned fabric that is a solid color

reverse method of braiding. The open edges on the right instead of to the left

second turn. LLR, LR, LLR (only used in a spiral rug)

set. A group of three adjacent loops including of one of each color, measured from one matching color loop to the next

sharp or square corner. Left-left-left-right

spiral. One continuous braid

splicing. Joining lacing thread together without a knot

tapering. Ending a continuous braid on a spiral rug

turn. Going around a corner (first turn; second turn)